Equivalent Measures

This table is designed to do the mathematics for you when you want to divide ingredients in a recipe.

Ingredient to Be Divided	¼ of	⅓ of	½ of	⅔ of
¼ teasp.	pinch*	pinch*	⅛ t	2 pinches*
½ teasp.	⅛ t	2 pinches*	¼ t	⅓ t
1 teasp.	¼ t	⅓ t	½ t	⅔ t
1 tablesp.	¾ t	1 t	1½ t	2 t
2 tablesp.	2¼ t	2 t	1 T + 1½ t	4 t
5 tablesp.	1 T + ¾ t	1 T + 2 t	2 T + 1½ t	3 T + 1 t
7 tablesp.	1 T + 2¼ t	2 T + 1 t	3 T + 1½ t	4 T + 2 t
¼ cup	1 T	1 T + 1 t	2 T	2 T + 2 t
⅓ cup	1 T + 1 t	1 T + 2⅓ t	2 T + 2 t	3 T + 1⅔ t
½ cup	2 T	2 T + 2 t	¼ c	5 T + 1 t
⅔ cup	2 T + 2 t	3 T + 1⅔ t	⅓ c	7 T + ⅓ t
¾ cup	3 T	¼ c	6 T	½ c

*Pinch is as much as can be taken between tip of forefinger and thumb. If ingredient is a liquid, use 4–5 drops per pinch.

Abbreviations:
t = teaspoon   T = tablespoon   c = cup

◆CUTCO◆
Cook Book

By Margaret Mitchell
Director, Home Economics

Published by CUTCO DIVISION
Copyright 1972

Wear-Ever Aluminum, Inc.
Chillicothe, Ohio

*C*ooking, today, is different than ever before. To begin with, social, civic and recreational activities leave less time for cooking. In addition, home entertaining is again becoming very popular. This is true whether it is for two or twenty people. And, due to increased travel and special magazine features, wants and desires for different foods have increased.

The one thing about cooking that I hope never changes, however, is the individual personality of you, the cook. No matter what your tastes and likes are, these can and will be reflected in the type of table you set. We have tried to keep you in mind when we prepared the Cutco Cookbook. Rather than devote the entire book to a variety of recipes, we have attempted to be as comprehensive as possible in helping you plan and prepare interesting menus. Charts and guides were developed to help you buy, prepare and store food products.

A special section on entertaining might give you different and interesting ideas on how to make your next event—large or small—even better. We have even included conveniently located charts on can sizes, equivalent measures and substitutes. The only advice I would like to give you is this: look through the entire cookbook before you use it. This will give you a real good idea what the contents are and how you can best use the cookbook to your personal advantage.

Margaret M. Mitchell
Director, Wear-Ever Kitchens

◆CUTCO◆ French Chef's Knife

Directions for Use:

1. Place food to be chopped on chopping board.

2. Grasp handle of FRENCH CHEF'S KNIFE between thumb and forefinger with fingers following curve of handle.

3. Place tip of blade on cutting board at a 45 degree angle with surface of board.

4. Place thumb and fingers of other hand on tip of blade, holding it firmly to the board.

5. Move knife down and up in a rocking motion keeping tip of blade on the board; at the same time move knife back and forth across board in a quarter circle.

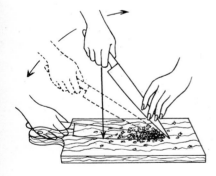

Note:

1. When dicing celery, carrots, green beans, etc., place 8–10 pieces lengthwise on chopping board.

2. Hold pieces firmly with left hand.

3. Slowly push pieces under blade of FRENCH CHEF'S KNIFE, at same time move knife down and up in rocking motion.

Uses:

● Chopping greens (cabbage, celery, lettuce, endive, radishes, watercress, romaine) for salads.

● Dicing apples, pears, canned fruits.

● Preparing potatoes for French frying, hashed brown, scalloping.

● Dicing celery, carrots, onions, potatoes, all greens, peppers, green beans, turnips, parsnips, beets.

● Cubing bread for stuffing, puddings.

● Chopping nuts, raisins, candied fruits.

● Dicing cooked meats, fowl.

◆CUTCO◆ Butcher Knife

Directions for Use:

1. Place food to be cut on cutting board.

2. Grasp handle of BUTCHER KNIFE between thumb and forefinger with fingers following curve of handle.

3. Place portion of blade nearest to handle of BUTCHER KNIFE on food to be cut.

4. Pull back on knife at same time pressing downward, using a long firm stroke. Never cut through bone.

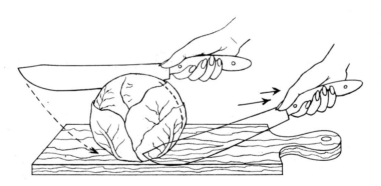

Uses:

● Disjointing chicken, turkey, duck.

● Preparing pork loin; preparing spare ribs.

● Cutting short ribs from rib roast.

● Cutting chuck roast, rump, brisket.

● Cutting squash, pumpkin, rutabaga, cabbage, watermelon, sweet potatoes.

● Cutting lobster, crawfish.

● Removing head of fish, scaling fish.

◆CUTCO◆ Trimmer

Directions for Use:

1. Grasp handle of the TRIMMER between thumb and forefinger with fingers following curve of handle.

2. The TRIMMER is held in the same position regardless of the task: slicing, cutting, trimming, coring, boning, scraping.

Uses:

● Slicing tomatoes, oranges, cucumbers, hard boiled eggs, green peppers, peaches, pears.

● Cutting and sectioning grapefruit, oranges.

● Making celery curls, carrot sticks, cutting corn from cob.

● Trimming cauliflower, broccoli.

● Peeling pineapple, grapefruit, oranges, melons, eggplant, squash.

● Coring lettuce, green peppers.

● Boning rib roasts, steak, fish, fowl.

● Removing tough outer rind, gristle and excess fat from steaks, chops, roasts; blood vessels from heart, membrane from sweetbreads, kidneys.

● Scraping steaks, roasts, skin of fish before cooking.

● Removing fins from fish; pinfeathers from chickens.

● Gashing edges of steaks, chops, ham slices before broiling.

◆CUTCO◆ Petite Carver

Directions for Use:

1. Place food to be cut or sliced on cutting board.

2. Grasp handle of PETITE CARVER between thumb and forefinger with fingers following curve of handle.

3. Place portion of blade of PETITE CARVER nearest to handle on food to be sliced.

4. Pull back on knife with a long sweeping stroke, at the same time exerting a gentle downward pressure. Never use a sawing motion.

Uses:
- Carving steaks, small roasts, hams.
- Carving chicken, duck, game, small turkeys.
- Halving grapefruit, slicing pineapple, small melons.
- Slicing eggplant, squash.
- Cutting layer cake.

◆CUTCO◆ Carving Knife

Directions for Use:

1. Place meat or fowl to be carved on platter.

2. Grasp handle of CARVING KNIFE between thumb and forefinger with fingers following curve of handle.

3. Grasp handle of CARVING FORK in the same manner in other hand; insert tines in meat or fowl.

4. Place portion of blade of CARVING KNIFE nearest to handle on meat or fowl to be carved.

5. Pull back on knife at same time pressing firmly downward to cut through the meat, using a long sweeping stroke rather than a sawing motion.

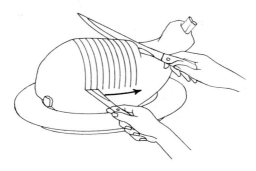

Uses:
● Carving large roasts with bone such as standing ribs of beef, leg of lamb, pork loin, baked ham.
● Carving turkey, chicken, duck, wild game.

◆CU⊤CO◆ The Slicer

Directions for Use:

1. Place boneless meat or other food to be sliced on cutting board.

2. Grasp handle of THE SLICER between thumb and forefinger with fingers following curve of the handle.

3. Place portion of blade of THE SLICER nearest to handle on food to be sliced.

4. Pull back on knife with a long sweeping stroke, at the same time exerting gentle downward pressure. Never use a sawing motion.

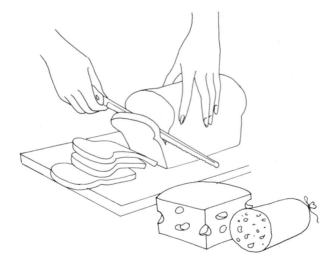

Uses:

● Slicing rolled roasts, white meat of fowl, ham loaf, ham and other boneless meats.

● Slicing all kinds of cheese, eggplant.

● Cutting bread, sandwiches, layer cake.

● Shredding cabbage, lettuce.

◆CUTCO◆ Carving Fork and Turning Fork

Directions for Use:
Grasp handle of the CARVING FORK or TURNING FORK between thumb and forefinger with fingers following curve of handle.

CARVING FORK:
● Turning large roasts or turkeys.
● Holding large roasts or turkeys in place during carving.

TURNING FORK:
● Turning bacon, liver, steaks, chops, fried chicken, ham, fish.
● Serving meats, fish or fowl.
● Removing beets, turnips, ruta-baga, sauerkraut, corn on the cob, spinach from cooking utensil.
● Stirring foods in fry pan while sautéeing.
● Tossing ingredients together, such as, crumb mixtures, meat loaf mixtures.

TURNING FORK AND CARVING FORK TOGETHER:
● Lifting large roasts or turkey from the roasting pan to the serving platter.

◆CUTCO◆ Paring Knife

Directions for Use:
1. Hold food to be pared firmly in fingers and thumb of left hand.
2. Lay PARING KNIFE across fingers of right hand with cutting edge of knife pointed to the left. Allow fingers to follow the curve of the handle.
3. Place the thumb of the right hand gently against food to be pared.
4. Make a cut through the skin of the food to be pared; continue cutting a thin layer of the skin using the right thumb to rotate the food and guide the blade of the knife. (Reverse procedure if left-handed.)

Uses:
● Paring potatoes, apples, cucumbers, peaches, pears, parsnips, turnips, rutabaga.

● Removing roots and stems from carrots, beets, rhubarb, radishes, spinach, cauliflower, celery.

● Scaling asparagus, trimming Brussels sprouts, scraping carrots.

● Cutting eyes from potatoes and blemishes from fruits.

● Pitting plums, peaches, nectarines, pomegranates.

● Seeding and skinning grapes.

● Making radish roses, celery curls, pickle fans.

● Removing black line from shrimp.

● Removing stomach sac from lobster.

◆CU̅TCO◆ Spatula Spreader

Directions for Use:
Grasp handle of the SPATULA SPREADER between thumb and fore-finger with fingers following curve of handle.

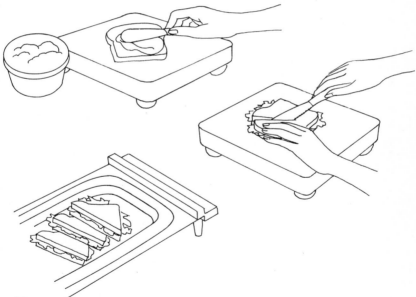

Uses:
- Icing cakes, cookies.
- Spreading sandwiches with butter and sandwich fillings.
- Cutting sandwiches.
- Cutting and removing bar cookies from pan.
- Spreading tea sandwiches and canapes with filling.
- Perfect for lifting that first piece of pie from the plate.

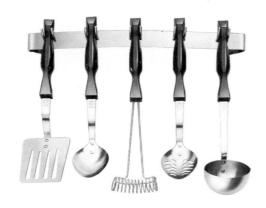

◆CUTCO◆
Kitchen Tool Set

Directions for Use:

1. Grasp handle of each KITCHEN TOOL between thumb and fore-finger with fingers following curve of handle.

2. When using MIX-STIR, slide coil back and forth across bottom of pan or bowl for fast, efficient, easy stirring, mixing, beating and blending.

Uses:

● **MIX-STIR**—mixing, beating, stirring, blending and whipping.

● **TURNER**—turning and lifting foods.

● **SOLID SPOON**—serving foods in liquids and sauces.

● **PERFORATED SPOON**—removing foods from liquids; skimming soups and stocks.

● **LADLE**—serving soups, gravies, beverages; pouring batters onto griddle.

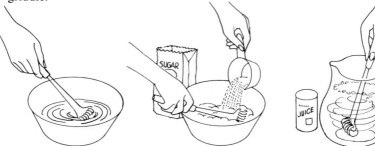

● **Mixes and Beats**—gravies, sauces, batters, puddings, fillings, candies, frostings.

● **Stirs and Blends**—flour and sugar into egg whites, sugar into whipped cream, soups and chowders.

● **Whips and Aerates**—milk shakes, eggs, toppings, fruit juices, instant puddings, instant potatoes.

◆CUTCO◆ Kitchen Shears

The KITCHEN SHEARS is the perfect tool for many cutting jobs around the kitchen. They come apart for easy cleaning.
The KITCHEN SHEARS simplifies the job of chopping many foods, such as parsley—merely hold the leaves of a sprig of parsley together and snip. When cutting sticky type foods such as marshmallows, dried and candied fruits—merely dip blades into granulated sugar several times while cutting to prevent food from sticking to them.

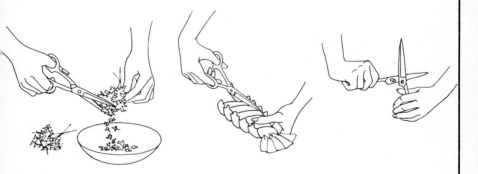

Uses:
- Snipping parsley.
- Cutting marshmallows.
- Cutting dried dates, figs, apricots, etc.
- Cutting candied fruits.
- Snipping shell on lobster tails.
- Cutting skin from chicken.
- Snipping top edge of grapefruit and orange halves for decorative effect.

◆CUTCO◆ Meat Knives

Directions for Use:
Grasp handle of the MEAT KNIFE between thumb and forefinger with fingers following curve of handle.

Uses:
Styled to complement the finest china and silver in your dining room and to be equally at home in your kitchen or at the barbecue grille. For cutting all types of steaks, chops, roasts, fowl.

Wear-Ever Fondue Set

Discover Fondue—the simple, convenient and fashionable way of cooking at the table; an elegant way to entertain friends and family.

A fondue pot is one of the few communal eating containers still in use in the Western world. The Swiss originated the fondue in the early days. Since that time, the fondue has been expanded to include many things.

As the custom continues today, we find people in the United States and other parts of the world gathering around the communal fondue pot enjoying all types of fondues. For instructions on how to prepare fondues, see Fondue Recipes on pages 111–115.

Combo Servers

Cutco's unique COMBO-SERVERS are the perfect companion pieces for elegant dining or an informal buffet table. Their contemporary design and attractive combination of wood, anodized aluminum and ceramic material makes them ideal for the following multi uses . . .

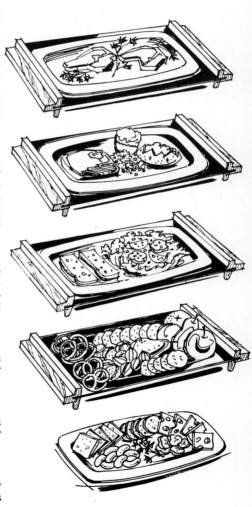

● **Individual Steak and Chop Platter**

Prepare steaks or chops in the usual manner. Preheat ceramic platters in oven for 10 minutes at 400°–425° F. (or place in oven for 5 minutes while steaks or chops are broiling). Place preheated platters in aluminum cradles; place steaks or chops on platters; garnish and serve. The meat will sizzle when placed on a hot platter. (Note —Platters should be preheated in oven only—never use on range top.)

● **Hot Food Server**

Preheat ceramic platter in oven about 10 minutes at 350° F. (or 15–20 minutes at 200° F.) just before serving. Place preheated platters in cradles; use for meat and vegetable course. Ideal for serving TV dinners.

● **Cold Food Server**

For cold dishes and salads, place food on platter and store in refrigerator. When ready to serve, platters may be used alone or placed in aluminum cradle.

● **Snack Tray**

Fill the aluminum cradle with pretzels, crackers, cookies, nuts or assorted fresh whole fruits.

● **Auxiliary Serving Tray**

Use ceramic platter alone as a small meat or vegetable dish or for relishes, fruit, salads, etc.

● **Buffet Serving**

Place COMBO-SERVERS side by side on table. Fill ceramic platters with relishes, cold cuts, cheese, salad, etc. The aluminum cradle alone makes a handsome bread or snack tray.

Menu Suggestions

ENTRÉE	APPETIZER	STARCHY FOOD	OTHER VEGETA
Roast Beef	Consommé	Golden Potato Wedges	Stuffed Artich
Delicious Meat Balls	Onion Soup	Cottage Potatoes	Chinese Green Bean
Swiss Steak	Tomato Juice	Au Gratin Potatoes	Browned Carr
Beef Burgundy	Fruit Cup	Parsley Rice	Spinach
Corned Beef	Clear Soup	Boiled Potatoes	Cabbage Wed
Roast Leg of Veal	Tomato Juice	Mashed Potatoes	Mushroom Baked in Fo
Wiener Schnitzel	Consommé	Buttered Noodles	Corn Curry
Exotic Greek Stew	Vegetable Juice	Steamed Rice	Buttered Bee
Sesame Veal	German Lentil Soup	Noodle Pudding	Brussels Spro
Veal Loaf	Creamed Vegetable Soup	Glazed Sweet Potatoes	Creamed Oni

BREAD	ACCOMPANIMENT	SALAD	DESSERT
Soft Rolls	Celery-Olives	Jellied Vegetable	Rhubarb Custard Pie
French Bread	Tomato Wedges	Lettuce with Roquefort	Coconut Cake
Hard Rolls	Spice Peach	Mixed Green	Canadian Apple Kuchen
Lt Rye Rolls	Celery Hearts	Lettuce and Tomato	Gingerbread with Nutmeg Sauce
Poppyseed Rolls	Mustard Sauce	Head Lettuce	Raspberry Cream Parfait
Muffins	Currant Jelly	Cucumbers in Cream	Deep Dish Apple-Cheese Pie
Hard Rolls	Toasted Almonds	Cole Slaw	Ice Cream
Rye Bread	Pickle Relish	Molded Vegetable	Chocolate Pudding
Biscuits	Celery-Olives	Tossed Green	Hot Fruit Medley
berry Muffins	Tomato Sauce	Head Lettuce	Southern Pecan Pie

Menu Suggestions

ENTRÉE	APPETIZER	STARCHY FOOD	OTHER VEGETA
Roast Leg of Lamb	Fruit Cup	Baked Potato	Stuffed Zucchini Bo
Maggie's Lamb Chops	Apricot Nectar	Hashed Browned Potatoes	Spanish Green Pea
Lamb Patties	Celery Soup	Home Fries	Eggplant-Tom Casserole
Grecian Lamb Balls	Tomato Juice	Rice	Baked Aspara
Fry Pan Kebabs	Vegetable Juice	Toast Points	Souffléed Caulifiowe
Baked Ham	Gazpacho	Escalloped Potatoes	Green Bean Almonds
Glazed Ham Balls	Consommé	Baked Sweet Potato	Buttered Pe
Roast Pork Tenderloin	Split Pea Soup	Wild Rice	Asparagus a la King
County Kerry Pork Chops	Tomato Juice	Lima Beans	Carrots in Sa
Spareribs	Vegetable Soup	Boiled Potatoes	Sauerkraut

BREAD	ACCOMPANIMENT	SALAD	DESSERT
ead Sticks	Mint Sauce	Jellied Vegetable	Nut Pie with Ice Cream
ard Rolls	Currant Jelly	Lettuce and Tomato	Black Bottom Pie
hite Bread	Brown Gravy	Cole Slaw	Spice Cake
orn Sticks	Sweet Pickles	Grated Carrot	Blueberry Buckle
oft Rolls	Steak Sauce	Head Lettuce	Fruit Curry
Biscuits	Raisin Sauce	Tossed Green	Blueberry Pie
aisin Bread	Celery Hearts	Cottage Cheese	Danish Apple Cake
ornbread	Broiled Half Peach	Sauerkraut Relish	Lemon Sherbert
alt Sticks	Apple Rings	Tossed Green	Strawberry Sundae
mpernickel	Spiced Crab Apple	Tomato	Butterscotch Pudding

Menu Suggestions

ENTRÉE	APPETIZER	STARCHY FOOD	OTHER VEGETA
Roast Turkey	Vegetable Juice	Bread Stuffing	Creamed Oni
Cornish Hen	Tomato Soup	Wild Rice Stuffing	Asparagus
Mexican Braised Duck	Jellied Consommé	Sweet Potato Balls	Broccoli
Chicken Mornay	Tomato Juice	Golden Potato Wedges	Spanish Green Pea
Salmon Casserole	Beef Broth	Lima Beans	Buttered Be
Belgium Baked Codfish	Noodle Soup	Baked Potato	Stewed Toma
Halibut Supreme	Chicken Soup	French Fried Potatoes	Peas and Car
Heart	Asparagus Soup	Dublin Cheese and Potato Pie	Stewed Toma
Kidneys	Orange Sections	Boiled Potatoes	Spinach
Liver	Tomato Bouillon	Creamed Potatoes	Fried Eggpl

BREAD	ACCOMPANIMENT	SALAD	DESSERT
oft Rolls	Turkey Gravy	Cranberry Orange	Mince Meat Pie
ard Rolls	Cranberry Sauce	Frozen Fruit	Paradise Pizza
orn Sticks	Stewed Fruit	Celery Hearts	Cheese Cake
Biscuits	Pickles-Olives	Peach Melba	Rum Balls
elba Toast	Lemon Cucumber Sauce	Tossed Green	Spice Cake
Iard Rolls	Corn Relish	Head Lettuce	Apple Strudel
arlic Sticks	Tomato Wedges	Tossed Green	Cardamom Loaf
ioft Rolls	Celery Sticks	Orange Cucumber	Cottage Cheese Cookie Sticks
asted Rolls	Spanish Sauce	Confetti Relish Mold	Apple Pie
rn Muffins	Bacon	Pineapple and Cottage Cheese	Chocolate Cake

Meat Is Important

Down through the centuries meat has always been one of the most universally liked foods. It is the heart of the meal—the center around which the menu is planned.

There is pleasure associated with the eating of foods which have appeal to the eye and to the senses of taste and smell. Meat presents a mouth watering picture, and its aroma and flavor tempt even the most jaded appetite.

Aside from its great palatability, meat is necessary to the daily diet because it is such a rich source of the highest quality protein. It also furnishes valuable amounts of health guarding vitamins and minerals such as iron, copper and phosphorus, which go into the making of good blood and bones.

Meat can always be fitted into the budget because the less tender cuts, which are the least expensive, are just as nutritious as the more expensive tender cuts.

NEED FOR VARIETY

While it is true menus should be planned to give the necessary daily food requirements, it is of equal importance that there is variety.

No article of diet lends itself more readily to variety in menu making than does meat. In addition to the many kinds and cuts of meats, there are hundreds of different methods of preparing and cooking each. Try different cuts, prepare them in different ways and serve a different kind of meat each day.

7 Methods of Cooking Meat and Poultry

There are seven specific methods of cooking meat and poultry. They may be cooked by roasting, broiling, panbroiling, panfrying, deep fat frying, braising and cooking in liquid. The cut of the meat or the age of the poultry usually determines the cooking method.

HOW TO ROAST

Tender cuts of beef, veal, pork or lamb and young birds may be roasted as follows:

1. Season as desired. It makes little difference whether a roast or bird is salted before or after cooking because when done, the salt has penetrated only to a depth of about one half inch.

2. Line shallow roast pan with Alcoa Wrap; place meat, fat side up, poultry breast side up on rack in pan.

3. Add no water; do not cover pan. Roasting is a dry heat method of cooking. If the pan is covered or water added, the meat or poultry will be steamed.

4. Roast at 300°–325° F. to desired degree of doneness.

5. If meat thermometer is used, insert into center of thickest meaty part of meat or bird, being certain end does not touch bone, fat or gristle.

HOW TO BROIL

Tender beef steaks, lamb or mutton chops, sliced ham or bacon, ground beef or lamb, and chicken parts, broiler-fryers or ducklings are suitable for broiling. Fresh pork chops and patties should be broiled slowly to insure complete cooking in center without drying on surface. Veal is seldom broiled.

Steaks and chops should be cut at least one half inch thick. Broiler-fryers and ducklings should be halved or quartered and brushed with butter. To broil:

1. Turn oven regulator to "broil." Preheat as directed by range manufacturer.

2. Line broiler pan with Alcoa Wrap; place rack in pan.

3. Place meat or poultry on rack 2–5 inches from the heat; the thicker the meat the greater the distance from the heat.

4. Broil until top side is thoroughly browned; season with salt, pepper.

5. Turn; brown second side; season; serve at once.

HOW TO PANBROIL

The same tender cuts of meat suitable for broiling may also be panbroiled.

1. Place FRY PAN or GRIDDLE over medium-high heat.

2. Preheat until a drop of water dances on the surface; add meat; reduce heat to medium. When the cold meat hits the hot pan it will stick but as it cooks and browns it will loosen itself. If juices start to cook out of the meat, increase heat slightly.

3. When meat is brown on one side, turn; brown second side. Do not cover and do not add water.

4. When meat is cooked to desired degree of doneness, season and serve at once.

HOW TO PANFRY

Comparatively thin pieces of tender meat, meat that has been made tender by pounding, cubing, scoring or grinding, or meat that is breaded, and broiler-fryers or chicken parts are best suited to panfrying which is the cooking of meat in a small amount of fat. To panfry:

1. Place FRY PAN over medium high heat; add small amount of fat—usually two tablespoons will be sufficient.

2. When fat starts to bubble or sputter, add meat or poultry; cook as in panbroiling.

HOW TO DEEP FAT FRY

This method of cooking is almost always used for breaded meats and poultry or for croquettes made from leftovers. To deep fat fry:

1. Use enough fat or salad oil to cover meat or poultry completely. Allow at least 3 inches between surface of fat and top of kettle so fat will not bubble over during frying.

2. Gradually heat fat to correct temperature using thermometer, or follow manufacturer's instructions when using electric fryer. Temperatures for deep fat frying of meat and poultry range from 300° to 375° F., depending upon the size of the pieces and whether it is cooked or uncooked.

3. Place a few pieces of meat in fry basket; lower slowly into hot fat; cook until brown and thoroughly done.

4. Raise basket; let meat drain; repeat above procedure until all servings are cooked.

5. Fat may be used again if it is strained and stored in refrigerator.

HOW TO BRAISE

Braising, also known as pot roasting, is the method most frequently used for cooking the less tender cuts of meat or older birds. Some tender cuts are also better if braised. These include pork chops, pork steaks, pork cutlets, veal chops, veal steaks, veal cutlets, chicken legs and thighs. To braise:

1. Brown meat on all sides as in panfrying.

2. Season with salt and pepper.

3. Add little or no water; cover tightly.

4. Reduce heat to low; cook until tender, turning frequently. (Meats will cook in their own juices.) May also be done in an oven at 300°–325° F. in covered utensil.

HOW TO COOK IN LIQUID

Stewing, or cooking in liquid, is a method for less tender cuts of meat and stewing chickens. Browning of large cuts or whole birds is optional, however, it does develop flavor and improve color. To cook in liquid:

1. Brown meat on all sides in hot fat.

2. Add just enough water, stock or vegetable juice to cover meat or poultry.

3. Season as desired; cover; simmer until tender.

4. Add vegetables just long enough before serving to be cooked.

5. If the meat is to be served cold, let it cool and then refrigerate in the stock in which it was cooked. The meat is more flavorful and juicy and it will shrink less if cooled in its stock.

Buying Guide for Meat, Poultry

Meat	Amount to Allow Per Serving (Ready to Cook)
BEEF, VEAL, PORK, LAMB	Roast, boned and rolled—¼ pound Roast, with bone—½ to ¾ pound Ground—¼ pound Boneless, for stewing—¼ pound For meat stock—3 pounds raw meat to 1 gallon stock
BEEF	Steaks, without bone—⅓ to ½ pound Steaks, with bone—½ to ¾ pound Canned, cooked, boneless meats—3 ounces Short Ribs—½ to 1 pound Chipped dried beef—1½ ounces
VEAL	Chops, thick—⅓ to ½ pound Steak or Cutlet—¼ to ⅓ pound
PORK, FRESH	Chops, thick—½ to ¾ pound Spareribs—¾ to 1 pound Sausage—¼ pound
PORK, SMOKED	Whole ham—½ pound Ham Slice—⅓ pound Bacon—3 to 4 strips (18-20 per pound)
LAMB	Chops, thick—⅓ to ¾ pound Shanks—½ to 1 pound
VARIETY MEATS	Brains—¼ pound Hearts—¼ pound Kidneys—1 veal or lamb kidney, ¼ beef kidney Livers—¼ pound Oxtails—½ to ¾ pound Sweetbreads—¼ Tongue—¼ pound Tripe—¼
POULTRY	Chicken Broiler-Fryer—¼ to ½ bird Roasting, Stewing, Frying—¾ to 1 pound Turkey under 12 pounds—¾ to 1 pound over 12 pounds—½ to ¾ pound Cornish Hen—1 bird (1 to 1¼ pounds) Duckling—¾ to 1 pound Goose—1 to 1½ pounds

Beef Chart

Retail Cuts of Beef—Where they come from and how to cook them.

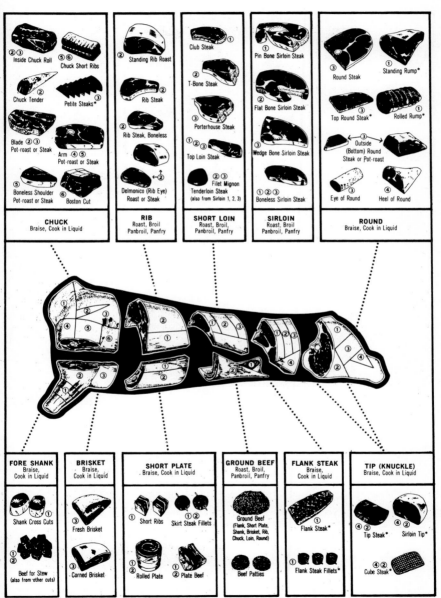

CHUCK
Braise, Cook in Liquid

Inside Chuck Roll ②③
Chuck Short Ribs ⑤⑥
Chuck Tender ②
Petite Steaks* ③
Blade ②③
Pot-roast or Steak
Arm ④⑤
Pot-roast or Steak
Boneless Shoulder ⑤
Pot-roast or Steak
Boston Cut ⑥

RIB
Roast, Broil
Panbroil, Panfry

Standing Rib Roast ②
Rib Steak ②
Rib Steak, Boneless ②
Delmonico (Rib Eye) ③←②
Roast or Steak

SHORT LOIN
Roast, Broil,
Panbroil, Panfry

Club Steak ①
T-Bone Steak ②
Porterhouse Steak ③
Top Loin Steak ①②③
Filet Mignon ②③
Tenderloin Steak
(also from Sirloin 1, 2, 3)

SIRLOIN
Roast, Broil
Panbroil, Panfry

Pin Bone Sirloin Steak ①
Flat Bone Sirloin Steak ②
Wedge Bone Sirloin Steak ③
Boneless Sirloin Steak ①②③

ROUND
Braise, Cook in Liquid

Standing Rump* ①
Round Steak ③
Top Round Steak* ③
Rolled Rump* ①
Outside ③
(Bottom) Round
Steak or Pot-roast
Eye of Round ③
Heel of Round ④

FORE SHANK
Braise,
Cook in Liquid

Shank Cross Cuts ①
Beef for Stew ①②
(also from other cuts)

BRISKET
Braise,
Cook in Liquid

Fresh Brisket ③
Corned Brisket ③

SHORT PLATE
Braise, Cook in Liquid

Short Ribs ①
Skirt Steak Fillets ①②
Rolled Plate ①②
Plate Beef ①②

GROUND BEEF
Roast, Broil,
Panbroil, Panfry

Ground Beef
(Flank, Short Plate,
Shank, Brisket, Rib,
Chuck, Loin, Round)

Beef Patties

FLANK STEAK
Braise,
Cook in Liquid

Flank Steak* ①

Flank Steak Fillets*

TIP (KNUCKLE)
Braise, Cook in Liquid

Tip Steak* ④②
Sirloin Tip* ④②
Cube Steak* ④②

*May be Roasted, Broiled, Panbroiled or Panfried from high quality beef.   *Courtesy of the* NATIONAL LIVE STOCK AND MEAT BOARD

Veal Chart

Retail Cuts of Veal—Where they come from and how to cook them.

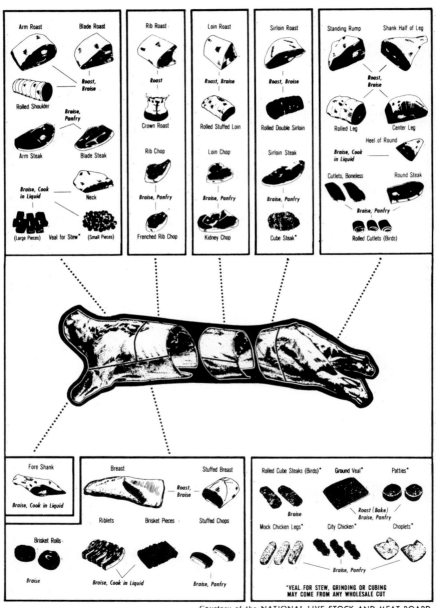

Arm Roast   Blade Roast

Roast, Braise

Rolled Shoulder

Braise, Panfry

Arm Steak   Blade Steak

Braise, Cook in Liquid   Neck

(Large Pieces)   Veal for Stew*   (Small Pieces)

Rib Roast

Roast

Crown Roast

Rib Chop

Braise, Panfry

Frenched Rib Chop

Loin Roast

Roast, Braise

Rolled Stuffed Loin

Loin Chop

Braise, Panfry

Kidney Chop

Sirloin Roast

Roast, Braise

Rolled Double Sirloin

Sirloin Steak

Braise, Panfry

Cube Steak*

Standing Rump   Shank Half of Leg

Roast, Braise

Rolled Leg   Center Leg

Heel of Round

Braise, Cook in Liquid

Cutlets, Boneless   Round Steak

Braise, Panfry

Rolled Cutlets (Birds)

Fore Shank

Braise, Cook in Liquid

Breast   Stuffed Breast

Roast, Braise

Riblets   Brisket Pieces   Stuffed Chops

Brisket Rolls

Braise   Braise, Cook in Liquid   Braise, Panfry

Rolled Cube Steaks (Birds)*   Ground Veal*   Patties*

Braise   Roast (Bake) Braise, Panfry

Mock Chicken Legs*   City Chicken*   Choplets*

Braise, Panfry

*VEAL FOR STEW, GRINDING OR CUBING
MAY COME FROM ANY WHOLESALE CUT

Courtesy of the NATIONAL LIVE STOCK AND MEAT BOARD

Lamb Chart

Retail Cuts of Lamb—Where they come from and how to cook them.

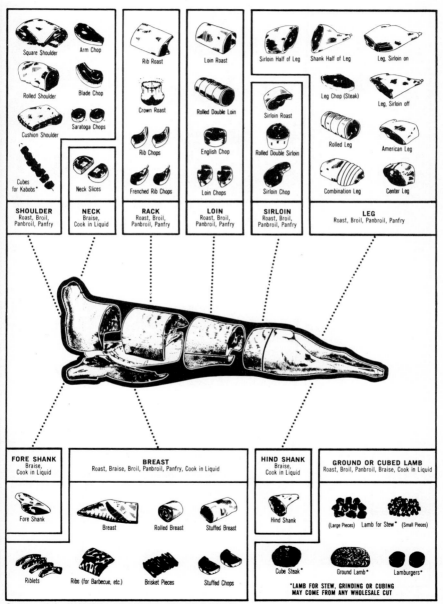

SHOULDER
Roast, Broil,
Panbroil, Panfry

Square Shoulder · Arm Chop · Rolled Shoulder · Blade Chop · Cushion Shoulder · Saratoga Chops · Cubes for Kabobs*

NECK
Braise,
Cook in Liquid

Neck Slices

RACK
Roast, Broil,
Panbroil, Panfry

Rib Roast · Crown Roast · Rib Chops · Frenched Rib Chops

LOIN
Roast, Broil,
Panbroil, Panfry

Loin Roast · Rolled Double Loin · English Chop · Loin Chops

SIRLOIN
Roast, Broil,
Panbroil, Panfry

Sirloin Roast · Rolled Double Sirloin · Sirloin Chop

LEG
Roast, Broil, Panbroil, Panfry

Sirloin Half of Leg · Shank Half of Leg · Leg, Sirloin on · Leg Chop (Steak) · Leg, Sirloin off · Rolled Leg · American Leg · Combination Leg · Center Leg

FORE SHANK
Braise,
Cook in Liquid

Fore Shank · Riblets

BREAST
Roast, Braise, Broil, Panbroil, Panfry, Cook in Liquid

Breast · Rolled Breast · Stuffed Breast · Ribs (for Barbecue, etc.) · Brisket Pieces · Stuffed Chops

HIND SHANK
Braise,
Cook in Liquid

Hind Shank

GROUND OR CUBED LAMB
Roast, Broil, Panbroil, Braise, Cook in Liquid

(Large Pieces) Lamb for Stew* (Small Pieces) · Cube Steak* · Ground Lamb* · Lamburgers*

*LAMB FOR STEW, GRINDING OR CUBING
MAY COME FROM ANY WHOLESALE CUT

Courtesy of the NATIONAL LIVE STOCK AND MEAT BOARD

31

Pork Chart

Retail Cuts of Pork—Where they come from and how to cook them.

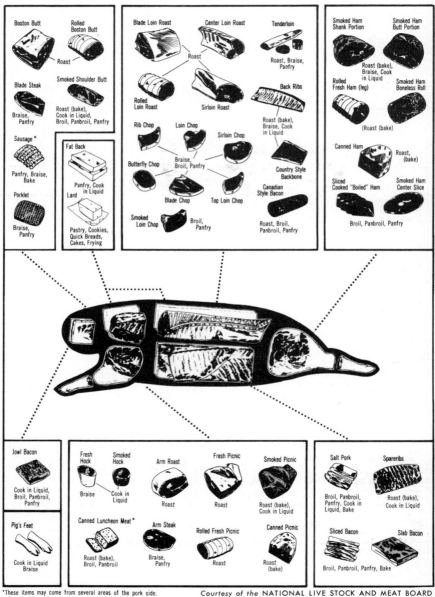

Boston Butt
Rolled Boston Butt
Roast

Blade Steak
Braise, Panfry

Smoked Shoulder Butt
Roast (bake), Cook in Liquid, Broil, Panbroil, Panfry

Sausage *
Panfry, Braise, Bake

Porklet
Braise, Panfry

Fat Back
Panfry, Cook in Liquid
Lard
Pastry, Cookies, Quick Breads, Cakes, Frying

Blade Loin Roast
Center Loin Roast
Roast
Tenderloin
Roast, Braise, Panfry

Rolled Loin Roast
Sirloin Roast
Back Ribs
Roast (bake), Braise, Cook in Liquid

Rib Chop
Loin Chop
Sirloin Chop
Braise, Broil, Panfry

Butterfly Chop
Blade Chop
Top Loin Chop

Country Style Backbone

Canadian Style Bacon

Smoked Loin Chop
Broil, Panfry

Roast, Broil, Panbroil, Panfry

Smoked Ham Shank Portion
Smoked Ham Butt Portion
Roast (bake), Braise, Cook in Liquid

Rolled Fresh Ham (leg)
Smoked Ham Boneless Roll
(Roast (bake))

Canned Ham
Roast, (bake)

Sliced Cooked "Boiled" Ham
Smoked Ham Center Slice
Broil, Panbroil, Panfry

Jowl Bacon
Cook in Liquid, Broil, Panbroil, Panfry

Pig's Feet
Cook in Liquid Braise

Fresh Hock
Smoked Hock
Braise
Cook in Liquid

Canned Luncheon Meat *
Roast (bake), Broil, Panbroil

Arm Roast
Roast

Arm Steak
Braise, Panfry

Fresh Picnic
Roast

Rolled Fresh Picnic
Roast

Smoked Picnic
Roast (bake), Cook in Liquid

Canned Picnic
Roast (bake)

Salt Pork
Broil, Panbroil, Panfry, Cook in Liquid, Bake

Spareribs
Roast (bake), Cook in Liquid

Sliced Bacon
Slab Bacon
Broil, Panbroil, Panfry, Bake

*These items may come from several areas of the pork side.

Courtesy of the NATIONAL LIVE STOCK AND MEAT BOARD

VARIETY MEATS
AND HOW TO COOK THEM

Brains—Braise, Broil, Panbroil, Panfry, Cook in Liquid

Hearts—Braise, Cook in Liquid

Kidneys
Beef, Pork—Braise, Cook in Liquid
Veal, Lamb—Broil, Panbroil, Braise, Cook in Liquid

Livers
Beef, Pork—Roast, Braise, Panfry
Veal, Lamb—Broil, Panbroil, Panfry

Oxtails—Braise

Sweetbreads—Braise, Broil, Panbroil, Panfry, Cook in Liquid

Tongues—Cook in Liquid

Tripe—Broil, Panfry

POULTRY SELECTION

Turkey

Fresh and Frozen
whole
halves and quarters
parts
Stuffed Frozen Whole
Frozen Boneless Rolls and
Roasts
uncooked
cooked
Frozen Breast of Young Turkey

Rock Cornish Game Hen

Frozen Whole
unstuffed
stuffed

Chicken

Fresh and Frozen
whole
halves
parts
cut up
Stuffed Frozen Whole

Capon, Duckling, Goose

Fresh and Frozen Whole

Care of Meat in the Home

Refrigerator Storage

The meat you buy should be properly cared for to insure its freshness. Keeping it clean and storing it at a low temperature goes a long way in lengthening the storage life of fresh meat and poultry. Remember, as the temperature goes up, storage life goes down.

Of course, you must also exercise some judgment in recognizing spoilage in fresh meat or poultry.

Signs of spoilage:

off-odor	loss of freshness
slippery surface	change in color

To insure freshness in meat and poultry, follow these suggestions for storage.

Steaks, Chops, Roasts—Meats wrapped in market paper should be unwrapped, covered loosely with Alcoa Wrap, stored in the coldest part of the refrigerator or in the compartment designed for meat storage. Storage should not exceed three days. Meats prepackaged for self-service may be stored in the refrigerator in the original wrapping if used within one to two days. Loosen ends of wrapping to allow circulation of air.

Ground Meats—They should be handled the same as steaks and chops, however, should be cooked within 24 hours for best eating quality.

Smoked or Cured Meats—Meats such as corned beef, bacon, hams, should be stored in their original wrappers in the refrigerator. For best eating quality, storage time should not exceed one week.

Variety Meats—Since variety meats such as liver, hearts, kidneys, sweetbreads are more perishable than other meats, they should be cooked and served within 24 hours of purchase.

Cooked Meats—They should be cooled, covered or wrapped tightly in Alcoa Wrap, and stored in the coldest part of the refrigerator or in the area designed for meat storage. Cooked meat will keep better if left in larger pieces and not cut until ready to use. Storage time should not exceed 5 days.

34

Poultry—Fresh poultry should be wrapped loosely to allow some air circulation. It should be stored in the coldest part of the refrigerator or in the compartment designed for meat storage. Storage should not exceed two days. Prompt cooking of the giblets is recommended.

Cooked poultry, stuffing, and any gravy should be cooled promptly, wrapped separately, then stored in coldest part of the refrigerator. Storage should not exceed three days.

Freezer Storage

There are a number of important facts to remember when freezing meats and poultry in the home. Of course, the sooner it is frozen after being purchased, the better.

● Use durable moistureproof wrap such as foil.

● Cover sharp bones with double thickness of foil.

● Wrap tightly and shape foil to surface of meat or poultry to eliminate all air.

● Use drugstore folds.

● Label with name, number of items and/or weight and date.

● Place packages in single layer on coldest part of freezer to freeze as fast as possible.

Steaks, Chops, Roasts—Package steaks and chops according to the number of servings needed. Wrap meats tightly in heavy duty Alcoa Wrap, separating individual servings by a square of foil, and using tight double folds to seal each package. Label packages noting date, cut and weight or number of servings.

Meats, prepackaged as fresh meat for self-service, may be frozen in the original package for short storage, one to two weeks. For long freezer storage, the original package should be overwrapped or rewrapped with Alcoa Wrap.

Recommended Maximum Storage Periods

Fresh Beef —6 to 12 months
Fresh Veal —6 to 9 months
Fresh Lamb—6 to 9 months
Fresh Pork —3 to 6 months

Ground Meats—Shape ground meat into patties or package in portions for loaves or other dishes. Season ground beef after thawing since the flavor of most seasonings is intensified upon freezer storage. Follow wrapping instructions for steaks, chops, roasts.

Recommended Maximum Storage Periods

Ground Beef —3 to 4 months
Ground Veal —3 to 4 months
Ground Lamb—3 to 4 months
Ground Pork —1 to 3 months

Smoked or Cured Meats—Recommended Maximum Storage Periods
Hams, ham slices, sausage . . . . .2 months
Frankfurters, bacon . . . . .1 month
Corned beef . . . . .2 weeks
Luncheon meats, canned hams . . . . .not recommended

Variety Meats—Brains, hearts, kidneys and beef or lamb livers may be frozen uncooked for 3 to 4 months; pork liver for 1 to 2 months.

Sweetbreads should be cooked, cooled, divided into portions before freezing. Storage should not exceed 4 months.

Preferred method for beef and veal tongue is to have them corned or smoked before freezing. Storage should not exceed 4 months.

Cooked Meats—They should be cooked, wrapped tightly in Alcoa Wrap, then frozen for not more than 2 to 3 months.

Poultry—Never freeze an uncooked stuffed bird or a roasted stuffed bird.

Fresh poultry may be frozen and held from 6 to 12 months. Cooked poultry slices or pieces covered with broth or gravy may be held frozen up to 6 months; when not covered with liquid use within 30 days.

Thawing Methods

Meats—Recommended methods:
1. in the refrigerator—in freezer wrapping.
2. at room temperature—in freezer wrapping.
3. during cooking.

Cook frozen roasts at 300° to 325° F., allowing ⅓ to ½ again as long as for cooking thawed roasts.

Poultry—Thawing whole birds at room temperature, unwrapped, is not recommended because of the possibility of contamination.

Recommended methods:
1. in the refrigerator, unwrapped, on a tray—requires 1 to 3 days.
2. with bird still in original water-tight wrap, thaw under cold running water, or immersed in cold water, changing the water frequently—requires 3 to 7 hours, depending on size of bird.

Time-Temperature Charts

ROAST BEEF
300°–325° F. Oven Temperature

Cut	Approx. Weight	Meat Thermometer Reading	Approximate Cooking Time
	Pounds	*Degrees F.*	*Min. per lb.*
Standing Rib	6–8	140 (rare) 160 (med.) 170 (well)	23–25 27–30 32–35
Standing Rib	4–6	140 (rare) 160 (med.) 170 (well)	26–32 34–38 40–42
Rolled Rib	5–7	140 (rare) 160 (med.) 170 (well)	32 38 48
Rib Eye (Delmonico)	4–6	140 (rare) 160 (med.) 170 (well)	18–20 20–22 22–24
Rolled Rump (High Quality)	4–6	150–170	25–30
Sirloin Tip (High Quality)..	3½–4	150–170	35–40

ROAST VEAL
300°–325° F. Oven Temperature

Cut	Approx. Weight	Meat Thermometer Reading	Approximate Cooking Time
	Pounds	*Degrees F.*	*Min. per lb.*
Leg	5–8	170	20–35
Loin	4–6	170	30–35
Rib (Rack)	3–5	170	35–50
Rolled Boned Shoulder	4–6	170	40–45

Time-Temperature Charts

ROAST LAMB
300°–325° F. Oven Temperature

Cut	Approx. Weight	Meat Thermometer Reading	Approximate Cooking Time
	Pounds	*Degrees F.*	*Min. per lb.*
Leg	5–8	175	30–35
Boneless Leg	3–5	175	35–40
Crown Roast	4–6	175	40–45
Rib (Rack)	4–5	175	40–45
Shoulder			
Bone in	4–6	175	30–35
Cushion Style	3–5	175	30–35
Rolled	3–5	175	40–45

FRESH PORK

325°–350° F. Oven Temperature

Cut	Approx. Weight	Meat Thermometer Reading	Approximate Cooking Time
	Pounds	*Degrees F.*	*Min. per lb.*
Loin			
Center	3–5	170	30–35
Half	5–7	170	35–40
End	3–4	170	40–45
Roll	3–5	170	35–45
Boneless Tip	2–4	170	30–35
Crown	4–6	170	35–40
Picnic Shoulder			
Bone in	5–8	185	30–35
Rolled	3–5	170	35–40
Boston Shoulder	4–6	185	45–50
Leg (fresh ham)			
Whole, bone in	10–14	185	30–35
Whole, boneless	7–10	170	30–35
Half, bone in	5–7	170	35–40
Tenderloin	½–1		45–60
Spareribs		Well done	1½–2½ hrs.

Time-Temperature Chart
BAKED HAM
300°–325° F. Oven Temperature

Cut	Approx. Weight	Meat Thermometer Reading	Approximate Cooking Time
	Pounds	*Degrees F.*	*Min. per lb.*
Ham			
(Cook before eating)			
Whole	10–14	160	18–20
Half	5–7	160	22–25
Shank portion	3–4	160	35–40
Butt portion	3–4	160	35–40
Ham			
(Fully cooked)			
Whole	10–14	130	10–15
Half	5–7	130	18–24
Loin	3–5	160	25–30
Picnic Shoulder			
(Cook before eating) ...	5–8	170	35
Picnic Shoulder			
(Fully cooked)	5–8	130	25–30
Shoulder Roll			
(Butt)	2–4	170	35
Canadian-Style			
Bacon	2–4	160	35–40

Time-Temperature Chart

POULTRY
The Tent Method—325° F. Oven Temperature

Type	Purchased Weight	Approx. Total Time—Stuffed*
	Pounds	*Hours*
Chicken	3	2½
	6	4
Capon	6	4
	8	4½
Turkey	8–10	3½–4¼
	10–12	4¼–4¾
	12–14	4¾–5½
	14–16	5½–6
	16–18	6 –6¾
	18–20	6¾–7½
	20–24	7½–8¾
Duck	3	2¼
	6	3¾
Goose	8	4
	11	4½

*NOTE—Times are for stuffed poultry. For unstuffed, deduct 3–5 minutes per pound.

Good to Know: When consulting the Time-Temperature Chart, keep in mind that meat and bone structure of poultry does vary. For this reason, times given are approximate and should serve only as a guide.

Start to test for doneness about one-half hour before bird is supposed to be done. Fowl is done when legs will move up and down freely. Another test is to press the thickest part of the drumstick between the fingers—meat should be soft. Protect fingers with piece of paper towel.

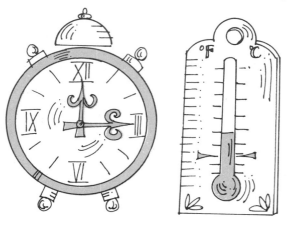

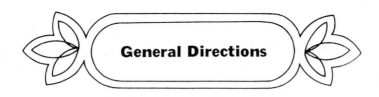

General Directions

ROASTS
Use Tender Cuts of Meat

1. Wipe meat with damp cloth to remove any small loose pieces of bone.
2. If desired, rub meat on all sides with the cut side of a clove of garlic.
3. Sprinkle with salt, pepper.
4. Line shallow roast pan with Alcoa Wrap; place meat fat side up on rack in pan.
5. If using a meat thermometer, insert into thickest part of meat being sure it does not touch bone, gristle or fat.
6. Add no water; do not cover pan.
7. Roast to desired degree of doneness. (See charts on pages 37–38.)

CROWN ROASTS—LAMB OR PORK

1. Have butcher shape two or more rib sections into "crown."
2. Cover ends of bones with cubes of bread or salt pork; remove these before serving.
3. Sprinkle with salt, pepper.
4. Line shallow roast pan with Alcoa Wrap; place meat on rack in pan.
5. Add no water; do not cover pan.
6. Roast to desired degree of doneness. (See charts on page 38.)

POT ROAST
Use beef rump or chuck; beef, veal or lamb shoulder.

4 pounds meat

1. Preheat ROUND ROASTER or 10-inch FRY PAN until a drop of water dances on the surface; add meat; brown thoroughly on all sides.
2. Sprinkle with salt, pepper.
3. Cover; cook over low heat 3–3½ hours or until meat is tender.
4. If desired, potatoes, carrots may be added during last hour of cooking.

BAKED HAM

If packer's wrapper or label contains directions for cooking, they should be followed. If you do not have such directions, use these:

1. Remove outside wrapper but do not remove rind.
2. Line shallow roast pan with Alcoa Wrap; place ham fat side up on rack in pan.
3. If using meat thermometer, insert into thickest part of meat being sure it does not touch bone, gristle or fat.
4. Add no water; do not cover.
5. Bake to desired degree of doneness. (See chart on page 39.)

TO GLAZE BAKED HAM

1. About 45 minutes before baking time is completed, remove ham from oven.
2. Remove rind with TRIMMER or KITCHEN SHEARS.
3. Cut or score fat surface into squares or diamonds using TRIMMER.
4. Stick whole cloves in center of each diamond.
5. Spread or baste with one of the following using SPREADER SPATULA or SOLID SPOON:

¾ cup canned crushed pineapple and ¾ cup brown sugar
   Pat brown sugar over ham; drizzle on honey or molasses.
1 cup brown sugar mixed with juice and grated rind of 1 orange
1 cup currant jelly or canned whole cranberry sauce, beaten with fork
1 cup orange, or orange grapefruit marmalade, beaten with fork
1 cup brown sugar combined with 1 cup juice from spiced or pickled peaches
1 cup puréed applesauce, apricots or peaches
1 cup brown sugar mixed with 1 teaspoon dry mustard, 2 tablespoons vinegar, fruit juice or cider or 1 teaspoon horseradish
1 cup brown sugar combined with ¼ cup fine soft bread crumbs
   Pat brown sugar over ham; place drained pineapple slices on top and maraschino cherry in center of each slice. Fruit may be fastened to ham with toothpicks and removed before serving. Use pineapple juice for basting.

GENERAL DIRECTIONS FOR TENT METHOD OF
ROASTING POULTRY

1. Line shallow roast pan with Alcoa Wrap.
2. Prepare bird according to recipe.
3. Place bird breast side up on rack in pan.
4. Fold piece of Alcoa Wrap, 4–5 inches longer than fowl, in half lengthwise to form Tent.
5. Place Tent over fowl, pressing one end lightly around drumsticks, other around neck opening.
6. Add no water; occasional basting of bird with drippings in pan is desirable, especially in dry areas; it improves flavor.
7. Roast according to chart on page 40.

ROAST CHICKEN, CAPON OR TURKEY

1. Clean, wash, dry bird.
2. Rub inside with salt, about ⅛ teaspoon per pound.
3. Fill cavity, neck opening with desired stuffing; pack lightly as stuffing swells during cooking.
4. Close cavity with skewers or poultry pins; lace with cord; pull neck skin back over stuffing; fasten with skewers or poultry pins to back of bird.
5. Tie a cord securely around the tail; then tie the ends of the legs to the same cord.
6. Bend tip ends of wings backward so they are held against back of bird.
7. Grease bird thoroughly with soft butter or margarine; sprinkle with salt, pepper.
8. Follow directions for Tent Method Roasting, above.
9. When bird is two-thirds done, cut cord around legs with KITCHEN SHEARS for complete cooking of the thick meated joints.
10. If bird is allowed to set 5–10 minutes after removal from oven it will be easier to carve.

ROAST DUCK

1. Clean, wash, dry duck.
2. Rub inside with salt, allowing ⅛ teaspoon salt per pound.
3. Stuff with desired stuffing or place 1 quartered apple, 1 quartered onion, 2 stalks celery in cavity; remove after roasting.
4. Follow directions for Tent Method Roasting, above.
5. Prick skin using TURNING FORK to allow fat to drain properly; remove excess fat from pan during roasting.

ROAST GOOSE

1. Clean, wash, dry goose.
2. Rub cavity with salt, allowing ⅛ teaspoon salt per pound.
3. To reduce fat: Place goose on rack in shallow open roasting pan lined with Alcoa Wrap; heat 15–20 minutes at 375° F. or until fat runs; dip out fat; repeat until fat ceases to drip.
4. Stuff cavity, neck opening with desired stuffing.
5. Prick fat on back, around tail and skin around wings, legs with TURNING FORK.
6. Follow directions for Tent Method Roasting, page 43.
7. If goose is very fat, remove excess fat from pan during roasting.

CORNISH HEN IN FOIL

1 Cornish hen (about 1 pound)	Melted butter or margarine
Wild Rice Stuffing	Salt

1. Clean, wash, dry bird.
2. Stuff bird with Wild Rice Stuffing; tie legs to tail.
3. Brush with melted butter; sprinkle with salt.
4. Place in center of a sheet of Alcoa Wrap; wrap tightly using double folds over top and at each end.
5. Place on rack in shallow pan.
6. Roast 1¼ hours at 425° F.; open foil for last 15 minutes.
7. One–two servings.

ROASTING HALF AND QUARTER TURKEYS

1. Rinse turkey with cold water; pat dry.
2. Skewer skin to meat along cut edges to prevent shrinking from meat during roasting.
3. Tie leg to tail; tie string around breast end to hold wing down.
4. Place turkey on rack in shallow roasting pan, skin side up; brush with butter.
5. Roast at 325° F. as follows:

Pounds	Hours
5–8	2½–3
8–10	3–3½
10–12	3½–4

44

Broiling Time Tables

BEEF
Turn meat after broiling ½ the time*

Cut	Thickness	Total Approximate Time (Minutes)*		
		Rare	Medium	Well Done
Club Steak	1 inch	8–10	11–13	13–15
	1½ inches	16–18	19–21	21–25
Fillet Mignon (or tenderloin)	1 inch	5–6	7–8	8–10
	1½ inches	8–10	11–13	13–15
	2 inches	11–13	15–17	17–19
Hamburgers	1 inch		8–10	10–12
Porterhouse Steak	1 inch	8–10	11–13	13–15
	1½ inches	16–18	19–21	21–23
	2 inches	27–30	34–36	36–40
Rib Steak	1 inch	8–10	11–13	13–15
Sirloin Steak	1 inch	10–12	12–14	14–16
	1½ inches	18–20	20–24	24–26
	2 inches	34–36	36–40	40–42
T-Bone Steak	1 inch	8–10	11–13	13–15
	1½ inches	16–18	19–21	21–23
	2 inches	27–30	34–36	36–38

LAMB
Turn meat after broiling ½ the time*

Cut	Thickness	TOTAL Approx. Time (Minutes)*
Patties from Ground Lamb	¾ inch	14–15
Rib or Loin Chops	¾–1 inch	12–14
Double Chops	1½ inches	20–25
	2 inches	36–40
English Chops	1½ inches	20–25
	2 inches	36–40
Shoulder Chops	¾–1 inch	14–16
	1½ inches	20–25

Broiling Time Table

PORK

Turn meat after broiling ½ the time*

Cut	Thickness	TOTAL Approx. Time (Minutes) *
SMOKED		
Ham Slice	½ inch	10–12
Ham Slice	1 inch	16–20
Loin Chops	½–¾ inch	15–20
Canadian-Style Bacon		
Sliced	¼ inch	6–8
Sliced	½ inch	8–10
Bacon		4–5
Ham Patties	1 inch	16–20
FRESH**		
Rib or Loin Chops	¾–1 inch	20–25
Shoulder Steaks	½–¾ inch	20–22
Patties	1 inch	20–25

**Fresh pork should be cooked slowly so that it is well done in the center but not dry on the surface.

GENERAL DIRECTIONS

Broiling Steaks, Chops, Ham Slices

1. Preheat broiler as directed by manufacturer.
2. Trim surplus fat from meat using TRIMMER.
3. Slash fat edge of meat at 2-inch intervals to prevent curling.
4. Line broiler pan with Alcoa Wrap; place broiler rack on pan; add meat.
5. Place broiler pan at least 1½ inches below heat—the thicker the meat, the greater the distance.
6. Broil to desired degree of doneness (See Charts on pages 45–46); season as desired.

BROILING MEAT PATTIES

1. Preheat broiler as directed by manufacturer.
2. Line broiler pan with Alcoa Wrap; place broiler rack on pan; add meat.
3. Place broiler pan at least 1½ inches below heat—the thicker the patties, the greater the distance.
4. Broil according to directions in charts on page 45; season as desired.

BROILING BACON

1. Preheat broiler as directed by manufacturer.
2. Line broiler pan with Alcoa Wrap; place broiler rack on pan; add bacon strips or slices.
3. Place broiler pan 3–3½ inches below heat; broil according to directions in chart on page 46.

BROILING CHICKEN PIECES

1. Preheat broiler as directed by manufacturer.
2. Line broiler pan with Alcoa Wrap; place broiler rack on pan; add chicken pieces, skin side down.
3. Brush well with melted butter or margarine.
4. Place broiler rack 3–3½ inches from heat; broil slowly so chicken just begins to brown at end of 10–12 minutes.
5. Turn; brush with melted butter every 10 minutes as browning increases.
6. Broil until tender and evenly browned—about 30 to 45 minutes depending upon size.

PANBROILING MEATS

1. Prepare steaks, chops, ham slices as directed for broiling; shape meat patties as desired.
2. Preheat FRY PAN or GRIDDLE over medium-high heat until a drop of water dances on the surface.
3. Drop meat into FRY PAN or GRIDDLE; brown thoroughly on one side.
4. Turn meat with TURNING FORK or TURNER SPATULA; brown second side; season as desired.

Note: When cold meat hits the hot pan or griddle, it will stick but as it browns it will loosen itself. Heat may be reduced to medium after meat has been added, however, if juices start to cook out of meat, increase heat slightly.

BRAISING PORK CHOPS

1. Prepare chops as directed for broiling.
2. Preheat FRY PAN over medium-high heat until a drop of water dances on the surface.
3. Add chops; reduce heat to medium; brown slowly on both sides.
4. Cover; cook over low heat 35–40 minutes or until tender.

PANBROILING BACON

1. Place bacon strips in cold FRY PAN or GRIDDLE.
2. Place over medium low heat; cook slowly, turning once with TURNING FORK.
3. For crisp bacon, drain off fat as it accumulates.

FRESH PORK SAUSAGES

1. Place links or patties in cold FRY PAN; add small amount of water; cover; bring to boil.
2. Simmer 5–10 minutes depending upon thickness; drain.
3. Cook uncovered over medium heat until golden brown and all pink has disappeared.
4. Drain off fat as it accumulates.

FRYING CHICKEN

1. Wash; clean chicken; cut into desired serving pieces using BUTCHER KNIFE and KITCHEN SHEARS.
2. For each pound of chicken use one of the following coatings:
   a. 2 tablespoons cornmeal, 2 tablespoons flour, ½ teaspoon salt, ⅛ teaspoon pepper, 1 teaspoon paprika blended together in paper bag.
   b. ¼ cup flour, ½ teaspoon salt, ⅛ teaspoon pepper, 1 teaspoon paprika blended together in paper bag.
3. Drop chicken pieces into bag; shake until pieces are coated.
4. Brown thoroughly on all sides in melted fat (part butter, part shortening or cooking oil) in 10-inch FRY PAN or ROUND ROASTER.
5. Cover; cook over low heat 35–60 minutes or until tender—time depends on size of chicken pieces.

OVEN FRYING CHICKEN

1. Prepare chicken for cooking as directed in Fried Chicken.
2. Place chicken pieces in shallow bake pan lined with Alcoa Wrap.
3. Melt ¼ pound butter, ½ cup shortening in 1-quart SAUCE PAN.
4. Spoon some butter mixture over chicken using SOLID SPOON; place in 350° F. oven.
5. Bake 1 hour or until tender, basting every 15 minutes with butter mixture.

BEEF HEART

1 5-pound beef heart

1. With PARING KNIFE remove fat, veins, arteries from cleaned heart.
2. Sauté sliced onion rings in ROUND ROASTER until lightly browned.
3. Add heart; brown thoroughly on all sides.
4. Add salt, pepper; cover with water.
5. Cover; simmer 2½–3 hours or until tender.
6. Thicken cooking liquid for gravy if desired.

SIMMERED BRAINS

1. Wash beef, veal, lamb or pork brains in cold water.
2. Soak ½ hour in salted water, allowing 1 tablespoon salt per quart water.
3. Remove membrane using TRIMMER.
4. Place in SAUCE PAN; add water to cover, 1 teaspoon salt, 1 tablespoon lemon juice or vinegar for each quart water.
5. Cover; simmer over low heat 15–20 minutes.
6. Drain; drop into cold water; drain again.
7. Serve with Mushroom, Tomato or Butter Sauce.
8. Allow four servings per pound.

SAUTEED BRAINS

1. Prepare Simmered Brains.
2. Dip into beaten egg, then fine dry crumbs or corn meal.
3. Sauté in butter in FRY PAN until brown.

BROILED BRAINS

1. Prepare Simmered Brains.
2. Brush with melted butter.
3. Broil 10–15 minutes, turning occasionally using TURNER SPATULA.
4. Serve with lemon wedges, broiled bacon, broiled tomatoes or Beet and Horseradish Relish.

LIVER AND ONIONS

1. Roll slices of liver in seasoned flour.
2. Sauté in butter until brown on both sides.
3. Sauté thinly sliced onion rings in another FRY PAN until golden brown.
4. Place liver on platter; turn onion rings into pan in which liver was cooked. Add 2 tablespoons hot water; stir using MIX-STIR to loosen sediment in pan; mix; pour over liver.

FRESH TONGUE

1 3–5 pound tongue

1. Wash tongue; place in ROUND ROASTER; cover with water; add seasonings.
2. Cover; bring to boil; simmer over low heat until tender, allowing about 50 minutes per pound.
3. Let tongue cool in cooking liquid.
4. Remove skin with TRIMMER; cut off thick end where small bones are apparent.
5. To serve cold: chill, slice thin using TRIMMER.
   To serve hot: reheat; serve with horseradish, barbecue or mustard sauces.

BEEF KIDNEY

1. Cut kidney crosswise into ¼-inch slices using TRIMMER.
2. Remove all fat, gristle; cut into small pieces.
3. Soak in cold water ½ hour; drain.
4. Cover with six cups boiling water; simmer uncovered 1 hour.
5. Cover; simmer ½ hour longer or until tender.
6. Thicken cooking liquid; season to taste.
7. Serve on toast.

BROILED KIDNEYS

1. Wash kidneys; cut in half with TRIMMER; remove fat, tubes with KITCHEN SHEARS.
2. Brush with melted butter or French dressing.
3. Sprinkle with salt, pepper.
4. Broil 5–7 minutes on each side.
5. Serve on toast with melted butter to which a little lemon juice has been added.

SWEETBREADS

1. Wash in cold water; let stand in cold water 20 minutes; drain.
2. Plunge into 2 quarts boiling water to which 2 tablespoons vinegar, 2 teaspoons salt have been added.
3. Cover; simmer 30 minutes.
4. Lift out with PERFORATED SPOON; plunge again into cold water.
5. Drain; remove fat, connecting tissues, fine membrane with TRIMMER; dry.
6. Split into halves lengthwise if very thick.
7. Serve Broiled or Creamed.

   To Broil:
   a. Brush with melted butter; sprinkle with salt, pepper.
   b. Broil until golden brown, about 5–7 minutes per side.
   c. Serve on toast.

   To Cream:
   a. Combine with medium white sauce to which 1½ teaspoons white wine, sherry or lemon juice have been added.
   b. Serve in patty shells.

TRIPE

1. Wash tripe; place in ROUND ROASTER; cover with water; add salt.
2. Cover; simmer over low heat 1 hour.
3. Drain; cut into serving pieces using TRIMMER.
4. Dip into beaten egg, then into dry bread crumbs.
5. Sauté in melted butter or margarine until nicely browned on both sides.

SAUTEED CHICKEN LIVERS

1. Wash; cut livers into halves with TRIMMER.
2. Sauté in butter or margarine until lightly browned.
3. Season with salt, pepper; stir in dairy sour cream if desired (1 cup per ½ pound livers).
4. Serve over cooked rice or on toast.

Entertaining

Successful entertaining is a highly creative exercise in pleasing other people. It is an art worth mastering, and it is fun.

Most of us enjoy having the company of others. The possibilities for party-giving are unlimited—brunches, luncheons, dinners, afternoon teas, morning coffees, Sunday night suppers, engagements, showers, anniversaries, teen-age parties, desserts and coffee, cocktail parties, barbecues.

When we think of entertaining and of having a party, we automatically think of food—what to serve? Here again, the possibilities are unlimited. The recipes on the following pages will be of great help to you in making that decision easier.

How to serve also requires some decision making, but can be a relatively simple task. The two main categories for the serving of food are the Sit-Down Meal and the Buffet Service. Both of these events may be as formal or as simple as you wish to make them.

The Sit-Down Meal

For the Sit-Down Meal, the food may be served in one of the following ways:

- *Food may be served at the table by the host or hostess.*

- *Food may be placed in serving dishes on the table and passed from person to person.*

- *Food may be placed on heated dinner plates in the kitchen and placed before each guest at the table.*

This Sit-Down Service is usually reserved for the heartier type meals such as brunches, luncheons, dinners, suppers, barbecues, although it can be effectively used for the dessert and coffee, showers, and so on.

The COMBO-SERVERS are the perfect companion pieces for the Sit-Down Meal. They can be preheated and used to serve each guest the meat and vegetable course attractively and piping hot. They can also be chilled and used to serve the cold meat and salad course. Alone, the ceramic platters make attractive service pieces for relishes and other side dishes.

The Buffet Service

The Buffet is a form of entertaining that is readily adaptable to a variety of occasions, and is flexible as to the number of guests. It can be as simple as a tray of sweet rolls and a pot of coffee placed on the coffee table in the living room for that morning coffee break with the neighbors. Or, a buffet can be developed using several trays of tiny sandwiches and cakes with a tea service arranged on the dining room table for that afternoon tea for the Women's Club.

The cocktail party is a natural for Buffet service. The more substantial hors d'oeuvres may be arranged attractively on the dining room table, while the lighter snacks, in small bowls and trays, may be conveniently placed around the entire entertaining area on smaller tables.

The Buffet may be expanded considerably so that it can be used to serve the more elaborate brunches, lunches, suppers and even a large dinner party. Regardless of the size or type of Buffet, the food should be arranged in appropriate serving order and the table itself be placed so the guests are able to move around it and reach the food easily. The table should be decorated with an attractive cloth and centerpiece, with plates, napkins and flatware conveniently placed prior to the arrival of guests. The dessert and coffee may be arranged on another smaller table in the dining area, or may be held in the kitchen and brought in at the appropriate time.

As with the Sit-Down Meal, the COMBO-SERVERS are a perfect addition to the Buffet. They can be used side by side in a line to make an attractive display for a variety of foods. Or the ceramic platters and cradles can be used separately for relishes, cold cuts, cheese, and for pretzels, crackers, cookies and breads.

When using the FONDUE SET, the COMBO-SERVERS can be used effectively:

- *to display the bread cubes for the cheese fondues.*
- *to display the meat cubes, slices or balls for the meat fondues.*
- *to display the dunkables for the dessert fondues.*

It is also important to plan the seating of the guests. If the living room or recreation room is to be used, traytables can be effectively used to augment available space on coffee or end tables. If you want to use card tables, it is necessary to have them preset with cloth, napkins, silverware and glasses. In good weather, a patio or terrace can be a most attractive setting for the party.

Now the stage is set for an adventure in good eating, whether it be with the family or entertaining guests.

Appetizers

Stuffed Mushrooms (France)

1 pound large fresh mushrooms
6 green onions
¼ cup butter or margarine
1 cup soft bread crumbs
1 cup canned crabmeat, flaked
1 teaspoon salt
⅛ teaspoon pepper
1 tablespoon ketchup
1 tablespoon lemon juice
3 strips of bacon
½ cup cream

1. Wash mushrooms; remove stems using PARING KNIFE; finely chop stems using FRENCH CHEF'S KNIFE.
2. Mince green onions using FRENCH CHEF'S KNIFE.
3. Melt butter in 8-inch FRY PAN over medium heat; add chopped mushroom stems, minced onions; sauté 5 minutes stirring with TURNING FORK.
4. Stir in bread crumbs, crabmeat; cook 2 minutes.
5. Add salt, pepper, ketchup, lemon juice; stir until well blended.
6. Stuff mushroom cups with above mixture; place in lightly greased bake pan.
7. Cut each strip of bacon in quarters using KITCHEN SHEARS; place two quarters criss-cross fashion on top of stuffing; fasten with toothpicks.
8. Pour cream around mushrooms.
9. Bake 25 minutes at 400° F.
10. Serve immediately.

Barbecued Spareribs

3 pounds spareribs
1 large onion
1 14-ounce bottle ketchup (1¼ cups)
¼ cup Worcestershire sauce
1 cup water
1 teaspoon salt
1 teaspoon chili powder

1. Cut spareribs into serving pieces using BUTCHER KNIFE.
2. Peel onion using PARING KNIFE; cut in thin slices using TRIMMER.
3. Lay spareribs in shallow 13 x 9-inch roast pan; lay onion slices on ribs.
4. Roast 30 minutes at 425° F.; discard onion slices.
5. In 2-quart SAUCE PAN, combine ketchup, Worcestershire sauce, water, salt, chili powder; bring to a boil, stirring with MIX-STIR.
6. Pour ¼ of barbecue sauce over ribs; roast 1 hour at 375° F., basting ribs every 15 minutes with remaining sauce using SOLID SPOON.
7. Eight servings.

Appetizers

German Ham Patties

1 medium onion
2 cups canned sauerkraut, well
  drained
1 tablespoon vegetable oil
1 pound ground ham
1 tablespoon prepared mustard
2 eggs, well beaten
1 teaspoon Worcestershire sauce
¼ cup flour
3 eggs well beaten
¾ cup packaged corn flake crumbs
4 tablespoons butter or margarine

1. Peel onion using PARING
   KNIFE; finely chop using
   FRENCH CHEF'S KNIFE.
2. Chop sauerkraut using FRENCH
   CHEF'S KNIFE.
3. Heat oil in 10-inch FRY PAN
   over medium-high heat; sauté onion 5 minutes stirring with TURN-
   ING FORK; remove onions with
   PERFORATED SPOON.
4. In a large bowl, combine onion,
   sauerkraut, ham, mustard, eggs,
   Worcestershire sauce, flour; mix
   well using TURNING FORK.
5. Cook 10 minutes in FRY PAN
   over medium-high heat, stirring
   frequently; cool.
6. Form mixture into small patties
   (1½ inches in diameter, ¼ inch
   thick); dip in beaten egg; coat with
   crumbs.
7. Melt butter in 10-inch FRY PAN
   over medium heat; fry patties, 10-
   12 at a time, until well browned
   on both sides; turn and remove
   with TURNER.
8. Three–four dozen patties.

Broiled Steak Rolls (Japan)

1 pound sirloin steak, ¼-inch thick
4 green onions
⅓ cup sherry wine
¼ cup Japanese soy sauce
2 teaspoons sugar

1. Cut steak in four sections using
   BUTCHER KNIFE; pound each
   section with edge of saucer or
   meat pounder until ⅛ inch thick.
2. Cut each section in half lengthwise using BUTCHER KNIFE.
3. Cut onions in half lengthwise using PARING KNIFE.
4. Lay onion strips on steak; starting
   with longest side, roll onion in
   steak; fasten with toothpick.
5. Combine sherry, soy sauce, sugar
   in bowl to make Teriyaki Sauce.
6. Brush steak rolls generously with
   Teriyaki Sauce; place on broiler
   pan.
7. Broil 3 minutes; turn using TURN-
   ER SPATULA; brush with sauce;
   broil 1 minute.
8. Remove toothpicks; cut in 1-inch
   long pieces using TRIMMER.
9. Makes about 2½ dozen hors
   d'oeuvres.

Gazpacho (Spain)

1 cucumber
2 green peppers
3 stalks celery
1 medium onion
3 hard cooked eggs
3 slices toast
6 tomatoes
1 cup canned tomato juice
1 10-ounce can condensed
  beef consommé
3 tablespoons wine vinegar
1 teaspoon salt

1. Pare cucumber using PARING KNIFE; quarter cucumber lengthwise; remove seeds using TRIMMER; cut in small cubes using FRENCH CHEF'S KNIFE.

2. Seed green peppers using TRIMMER; cut in cubes using FRENCH CHEF'S KNIFE.

3. Dice celery using FRENCH CHEF'S KNIFE.

4. Peel onion using PARING KNIFE; coarsely chop using FRENCH CHEF'S KNIFE.

5. Cube hard cooked eggs, toast using TRIMMER.

6. Place cucumber, green pepper, celery, onion, eggs, toast cubes in individual serving dishes; reserve for serving.

7. Purée tomatoes; combine puréed tomatoes, tomato juice, consommé, vinegar, salt, in bowl; blend using MIX-STIR.

8. Cover with aluminum foil; refrigerate several hours.

9. Serve each guest a bowl of soup to which he adds the accompaniments of his choice.

10. Four–six servings.

Creamed Vegetable Soup (Finland)

1 large carrot
1 stalk celery
1 medium potato
6 green onions
1 cup cauliflower buds
1 cup frozen peas, thawed
1 cup frozen green beans, thawed
3 cups water
2 teaspoons salt
2 tablespoons butter or margarine
1½ tablespoons flour
1 cup light cream
¾ cup milk
2 tablespoons chopped parsley
⅛ teaspoon thyme
  Dash white pepper
1 cup cooked, cleaned shrimp

1. Chop carrot, celery using FRENCH CHEF'S KNIFE.

2. Pare potato using PARING KNIFE; cut in small cubes using FRENCH CHEF'S KNIFE.

3. Slice onions using TRIMMER.

4. Combine carrot, celery, potato, onion, cauliflower, peas, beans, water, salt in 3-quart SAUCE PAN; bring to a boil; boil slowly, uncovered, 10 minutes.

5. Drain vegetables, reserving stock; set vegetables aside.

6. Melt butter in 3-quart SAUCE PAN; blend in flour using MIX-STIR; cook 1 minute, stirring constantly.

7. Gradually stir in vegetable stock, cream, milk; cook until thickened, stirring constantly.

8. Add vegetables, parsley, thyme, pepper, shrimp; cook until vegetables, shrimp are hot, stirring frequently; add more milk if soup is too thick.

9. Six–eight servings.

Note: This is a popular summer soup in Finland. It may be served for lunch or for a late supper.

Salads

Confetti Relish Mold

2 medium cucumbers
1 green pepper
6 green onions
12 radishes
8 beef bouillon cubes
4 3-ounce packages lemon flavored
  gelatin
1 quart boiling water
½ cup tarragon vinegar
2 teaspoons salt
1 quart dairy sour cream

1. Mince cucumbers using FRENCH CHEF'S KNIFE; do not pare.
2. Seed green pepper using TRIMMER; mince using FRENCH CHEF'S KNIFE.
3. Mince onions using FRENCH CHEF'S KNIFE.
4. Cut radishes in very thin slices using TRIMMER.
5. Dissolve bouillon cubes, gelatin in boiling water; add vinegar, salt; chill until partially set.
6. Add sour cream; blend thoroughly.
7. Add cucumber, green pepper, onions, radishes; blend.
8. Pour into 3-quart mold; chill until firm.
9. Fourteen–eighteen servings.

Frozen Fruit Salad

2 peaches, fresh (or 4 canned peach
  halves)
1 cup fresh strawberries
2 ounces shelled walnuts
8 maraschino cherries
1 pint dairy sour cream
¾ cup sugar
2 tablespoons lemon juice
⅛ teaspoon salt
1 9-ounce can crushed pineapple,
  drained
½ cup blackberries

1. Peel peaches using PARING KNIFE; cut in half; remove seed; slice using TRIMMER.
2. Hull strawberries; cut in half using PARING KNIFE.
3. Chop walnuts using FRENCH CHEF'S KNIFE.
4. Cut cherries in half using PARING KNIFE.
5. Combine sour cream, sugar, lemon juice, salt using MIX-STIR; blend well.
6. Fold in peaches, strawberries, walnuts, cherries, crushed pineapple, blackberries.
7. Pour into 9-inch or 8-inch square bake pan; freeze until firm.
8. Nine servings.

Salads

Orange-Cucumber Salad (Mexico)

4 oranges
1 cucumber
½ green pepper
½ onion
Lettuce
Vinegar and oil dressing

1. Peel oranges using TRIMMER; cut in ¼-inch slices using TRIMMER.
2. Score cucumber with fork (do not peel); cut in thin slices using TRIMMER.
3. Seed green pepper using TRIMMER; chop finely using FRENCH CHEF'S KNIFE.
4. Peel onion using PARING KNIFE; chop finely using FRENCH CHEF'S KNIFE.
5. Arrange orange slices, cucumber slices on bed of lettuce.
6. Sprinkle chopped green pepper, onion over oranges.
7. Serve with salad dressing.
8. Six servings.

Austrian Cucumber Salad

1 cucumber
1 medium onion
½ teaspoon salt
2 tablespoons vegetable oil
2 tablespoons white vinegar
⅓ cup sour cream
Paprika
Parsley, fresh

1. Peel cucumber, onion using PARING KNIFE; cut in thin slices using TRIMMER.
2. In small bowl combine cucumber, onion slices; sprinkle with salt.
3. Combine oil, vinegar; mix until blended; pour over cucumber, onion slices; cover; marinate 2 hours; drain well.

4. Add sour cream to cucumbers, onions; blend well; cover; chill 2 hours.
5. Serve on lettuce; sprinkle with paprika; garnish with chopped parsley.
6. Six servings.

Exotic Chicken Salad

2 whole cooked chicken breasts
3 stalks celery
1 large green pepper
2 cups grapes
2 cups canned pineapple chunks, drained
2 green onions
1 cup slivered almonds, toasted
⅔ cup mayonnaise
¼ cup light cream
1 teaspoon salt
⅛ teaspoon pepper
2 tablespoons vinegar

1. Cut chicken in large chunks using FRENCH CHEF'S KNIFE.
2. Slice celery diagonally using FRENCH CHEF'S KNIFE.
3. Seed green pepper using TRIMMER; mince using FRENCH CHEF'S KNIFE.
4. Cut grapes in half; seed using PARING KNIFE.
5. Cut pineapple chunks in half using PARING KNIFE.
6. Mince green onions using FRENCH CHEF'S KNIFE.
7. Combine chicken, celery, green pepper, grapes, pineapple, almonds in large bowl.
8. Combine onions, mayonnaise, cream, salt, pepper, vinegar; blend thoroughly.
9. Chill both mixtures separately.
10. Just before serving, blend together, tossing lightly; serve in lettuce cups.
11. Eight–ten servings.

Belgian Green Bean Salad

1 pound fresh green beans
2 large potatoes
4 green onions
2 tablespoons peanut oil
1¼ cup canned beef broth
6 slices bacon
3 tablespoons vinegar
¼ teaspoon thyme
⅛ teaspoon pepper

1. Clean beans; cut in 2-inch lengths using FRENCH CHEF'S KNIFE.
2. Pare potatoes using PARING KNIFE; cut into 1-inch cubes using FRENCH CHEF'S KNIFE.
3. Mince green onions using FRENCH CHEF'S KNIFE.
4. Heat oil in 10-inch FRY PAN over medium-high heat; add beans; sauté for 2 minutes, stirring constantly using TURNING FORK.
5. Add broth; cover; simmer 15 minutes.
6. Add potatoes; cover; simmer 30 minutes; drain.
7. In 8-inch FRY PAN, fry bacon until crisp; remove with TURNING FORK; drain on paper towels; reserve ⅓ cup bacon fat; crumble bacon.
8. Combine bacon fat, minced onions, vinegar, thyme, pepper; pour over beans, potatoes; toss until well blended.
9. Sprinkle crumbled bacon over each serving.
10. Six–eight servings.

Sauerkraut Relish Salad

2 stalks celery
1 canned pimiento
½ medium green pepper
1 medium onion
1 14-ounce can sauerkraut, well drained
⅓ cup vinegar
3 tablespoons salad oil
⅔ cup sugar
¼ cup water

1. Cut celery in diagonal slices using FRENCH CHEF'S KNIFE.
2. Chop pimiento using FRENCH CHEF'S KNIFE.
3. Seed green pepper using TRIMMER; chop using FRENCH CHEF'S KNIFE.
4. Peel onion using PARING KNIFE; cut in thin slices using TRIMMER; separate into rings.
5. Combine all ingredients in bowl; mix thoroughly using TURNING FORK.
6. Cover with Alcoa Wrap; (do not press foil onto mixture); refrigerate overnight.
7. Serve in lettuce cup.
8. Six–eight servings.

Note: Also excellent as a relish with sandwiches, meats.

Fresh Mushroom Salad (Finland)

1 pound fresh mushrooms
6 green onions
2 cups water
2 tablespoons lemon juice
½ cup dairy sour cream
¼ teaspoon sugar
1 teaspoon salt
Dash white pepper

1. Wash, slice mushrooms using TRIMMER.
2. Mince onion using FRENCH CHEF'S KNIFE.
3. Combine water, lemon juice in 2-quart SAUCE PAN; bring to a boil.
4. Add mushrooms; cover; simmer 3 minutes; drain on paper towels until cool.
5. In a small bowl, combine onions, sour cream, sugar, salt, pepper; mix well.
6. Add mushrooms to sour cream; blend well.
7. Serve immediately on lettuce.
8. Five–six servings.

Salads

Senate Salad

½ pound cooked shrimp
1 9-ounce package frozen
    artichoke hearts
1 grapefruit
2 medium tomatoes
2 stalks celery
¼ pound Cheddar cheese
10 ripe olives
6 green onions
2 quarts salad greens (romaine,
    leaf lettuce, escarole, cabbage,
    water cress)
1 3-ounce package lemon gelatin
1 teaspoon salt
½ teaspoon garlic salt
⅛ teaspoon pepper
1½ cups hot water
1 tablespoon vinegar
1 cup Italian dressing

1. Cut shrimp in 1-inch pieces using TRIMMER.
2. Cook artichoke hearts as directed on package; drain; cut each heart in half using TRIMMER.
3. Peel grapefruit; section using TRIMMER.
4. Dip tomato into boiling water for about 1 minute using TURNING FORK; peel, core using PARING KNIFE; dice using FRENCH CHEF'S KNIFE.
5. Cut celery in thin diagonal slices using FRENCH CHEF'S KNIFE.
6. Cut cheese in thin strips using TRIMMER.
7. Slice olives using PARING KNIFE.
8. Chop green onions, salad greens using FRENCH CHEF'S KNIFE.
9. Combine gelatin, salt, garlic salt, pepper; add hot water; stir until gelatin dissolves using MIX-STIR; add vinegar.
10. Pour into 9 x 5-inch loaf pan; chill until slightly thickened.
11. Press shrimp pieces, one inch apart, into thickened gelatin; chill until firm.
12. Combine artichoke hearts, Italian dressing; chill.
13. Combine grapefruit, tomatoes, celery, cheese, olives, onions, greens; toss together lightly in salad bowl; chill.
14. Just before serving, toss artichoke hearts, dressing with other ingredients.
15. Serve in lettuce cups; arrange shrimp squares on top.
16. Four large servings.

Swedish Herring Salad

2 salted herring
4 medium red onions
4 medium boiled potatoes
8 tart apples
6 medium cooked beets
3 small gherkin pickles
⅔ cup white vinegar
½ cup sugar
2 tablespoons capers
    Pepper
    Dairy sour cream
    Hard cooked eggs

1. Soak herring overnight in cold water; drain; split; skin; remove bone using TRIMMER; dice using FRENCH CHEF'S KNIFE.
2. Peel onions using PARING KNIFE; dice using FRENCH CHEF'S KNIFE.
3. Pare potatoes using PARING KNIFE; dice using FRENCH CHEF'S KNIFE.
4. Pare apples using PARING KNIFE; quarter; core using TRIMMER; dice using FRENCH CHEF'S KNIFE.
5. Dice cooked beets, gherkins using FRENCH CHEF'S KNIFE.
6. Combine herring, onions, potatoes, apples, beets, gherkins; mix well.
7. Add vinegar, sugar, capers, pepper; mix well.
8. Top with sour cream, garnish with sliced hard cooked eggs.
9. Eight servings.

Peach Melba Salad

    2 1-pound cans sliced peaches
    ¼ cup lemon juice
    2 3-ounce packages lemon gelatin
    2 cups hot water
    4 teaspoons milk
    ¼ cup mayonnaise
    2 3-ounce packages cream cheese,
         softened
    ¼ cup finely chopped pecans
    2 10-ounce packages frozen red
         raspberries, thawed
    ¼ cup lemon juice
    2 3-ounce packages raspberry
         gelatin
    2 cups hot water

1. *Peach Layer:* Drain peaches; combine peach syrup, lemon juice, enough cold water to make 2 cups.
2. Dissolve lemon gelatin in hot water; add syrup mixture; refrigerate until partially set.
3. Blend in peaches; pour into 3-quart mold; refrigerate until set.
4. *Cheese Layer:* Combine milk, mayonnaise, cream cheese; blend well using MIX-STIR; stir in pecans.
5. Spread cheese mixture over peach layer in mold using SPREADER SPATULA; refrigerate.
6. *Raspberry Layer:* Drain raspberries; combine raspberry syrup, lemon juice, enough cold water to make 2 cups.
7. Dissolve raspberry gelatin in hot water; add syrup mixture; refrigerate until partially set.
8. Blend in raspberries; pour over cheese layer in mold; refrigerate until set.
9. Unmold on bed of lettuce.
10. Fourteen–sixteen servings.

Nordic Potato Salad

    6 medium potatoes
    2 medium, tart red apples
    1 pickled herring
    1 medium dill pickle
    ⅔ cup mayonnaise
    1 teaspoon prepared mustard
    2 tablespoons sherry wine
    ½ tablespoon chopped chives
    2 teaspoons sugar
    1 teaspoon salt
    ⅛ teaspoon pepper

1. Boil potatoes with jackets on until tender; spear with TURNING FORK; remove skins using PARING KNIFE; cube while hot using FRENCH CHEF'S KNIFE.
2. Quarter apples; remove cores using TRIMMER; cube using FRENCH CHEF'S KNIFE.
3. Dice herring, dill pickle using FRENCH CHEF'S KNIFE.
4. Combine potatoes, apples in large bowl.
5. Combine remaining ingredients in small bowl; blend thoroughly.
6. Pour dressing over potatoes, apples; toss lightly to mix.
7. Cover; refrigerate several hours.
8. Six servings.

Entrees

Danish Open Sandwiches

The Danish open-faced sandwich is a typical Danish Lunch. It consists of a single slice of bread topped with a cold filling, attractively arranged and garnished. Although there are an endless variety of fillings, the bread is almost always a well-buttered dark sour rye (white bread with a hard crust is often used for fish or seafood fillings). The Danish sandwich is an excellent disguise for left-overs. Try some of the following combinations or create your own:

1. Sliced smoked salmon on a bed of scrambled eggs, garnished with a twisted cucumber slice. (Use TRIMMER.)

2. Thinly sliced cooked pork topped with strip of crisp bacon, twisted orange slice, pitted prune. (Use PETITE CARVER and TRIMMER.)

3. Thinly sliced cooked ham topped with scrambled eggs, chopped chives, sprig of parsley. (Use SLICER.)

4. Sliced cooked sausage patty topped with sliced boiled potato, sliced green onion, chopped pimiento. (Use TRIMMER and FRENCH CHEF'S KNIFE.)

5. Chopped cooked shrimp on bed of lettuce topped with shrimp sauce, twisted slice of lemon. (Use FRENCH CHEF'S KNIFE and TRIMMER.)

6. Ham salad topped with an orange section and twisted cucumber slice. (Use SPREADER SPATULA and TRIMMER.)

7. Sliced braunsweiger topped with piece of lettuce, strip of crisp bacon, slice of pimiento. (Use TRIMMER.)

8. Thinly sliced roast beef topped with tomato wedge, sliced pickle. (Use SLICER and TRIMMER.)

9. Marinated herring topped with onion rings. (Use TRIMMER.)

10. Curried macaroni and herring salad on bed of lettuce topped with twisted cucumber slice. (Use TRIMMER.)

11. Thinly sliced ham topped with sliced Swiss cheese, lettuce, cherry tomato. (Use PETITE CARVER.)

12. Grape jelly topped with sliced apples. (Use SPREADER SPATULA and TRIMMER.)

13. Peanut butter topped with crisp bacon slice, celery strips. (Use SPREADER SPATULA and TRIMMER.)

Entrees

Steak Eszterhazy (Hungary)

2 pounds top round steak, ½-inch thick
Salt, pepper
1 medium onion
1 stalk celery
1 small carrot
3 large sprigs parsley
1 medium carrot
2 gherkin pickles
⅓ cup flour
¼ cup vegetable oil
2 cups canned condensed beef consommé
¼ cup wine vinegar
6 whole allspice
2 bay leaves
⅛ teaspoon thyme
½ cup dairy sour cream

1. Cut steak into six equal portions using PETITE CARVER; sprinkle with salt, pepper.
2. Peel onion using PARING KNIFE; chop using FRENCH CHEF'S KNIFE.
3. Chop celery, carrot using FRENCH CHEF'S KNIFE.
4. Snip parsley using KITCHEN SHEARS.
5. Cut carrot in thin strips about 1½ inches long using FRENCH CHEF'S KNIFE.
6. Cut gherkins in thin strips about 1½ inches long using TRIMMER.
7. Coat steak with flour; pound with edge of saucer.
8. Heat oil in 10-inch FRY PAN over medium heat 4–5 minutes; quickly brown meat on both sides; remove with TURNER.
9. Sauté onion, celery, chopped carrot about 5 minutes stirring with TURNING FORK.
10. Stir in remaining flour (3–4 tablespoons) using MIX-STIR; slowly blend in consommé, vinegar; add allspice, bay leaves, thyme, chopped parsley.
11. Bring to boil; return meat to pan; cover; simmer 60–70 minutes.
12. Blend in sour cream; simmer additional 5 minutes.
13. Serve meat with gravy; garnish with carrot, gherkin strips.
14. Six servings.

Australian Curried Beef

1½ pounds boneless chuck
1 tart apple
1 medium onion
2 medium tomatoes
2 large sprigs parsley
2 tablespoons vegetable oil
1 teaspoon curry powder
1 tablespoon instant-type flour
1 10½-ounce can condensed beef bouillon
⅓ cup seedless raisins
1 tablespoon brown sugar
2 teaspoons salt
⅛ teaspoon pepper

1. Cut meat in thin strips 1½″ x½″ using PETITE CARVER.
2. Pare, core apple using PARING KNIFE; dice using FRENCH CHEF'S KNIFE.
3. Peel onion using PARING KNIFE; slice using TRIMMER.
4. Dice tomatoes using FRENCH CHEF'S KNIFE.
5. Snip parsley using KITCHEN SHEARS.
6. In 10-inch FRY PAN, brown meat quickly in oil over medium-high heat stirring with TURNING FORK.
7. Add apple, onion; sauté 2–3 minutes; stir in curry powder.
8. Add tomatoes, parsley, flour, bouillon, raisins, brown sugar, salt, pepper; blend well.
9. Cover; simmer 40–45 minutes until meat is tender.
10. Six servings.

Argentine Beef Pie

Pastry
2¼ cups sifted all-purpose flour
½ cup sugar
½ teaspoon salt
½ cup butter or margarine
2 egg yolks, slightly beaten
¼ cup water or Muscatel wine
Filling
2 medium potatoes
1 carrot
1 medium onion
1½ pounds cooked beef roast
½ teaspoon salt
1 10¾-ounce can beef gravy
⅓ cup raisins
½ teaspoon cinnamon
¼ teaspoon ground cloves
½ teaspoon oregano
⅛ teaspoon pepper
1 can (1 lb. 13 oz.) peach halves,
    drained
2 egg whites
2 tablespoons sugar

Pastry
1. Sift together flour, sugar, salt into bowl.
2. Cut in butter with pastry blender or 2 knives until mixture resembles coarse meal.
3. Add egg yolks; quickly blend in with fork.
4. Add water by tablespoons blending with fork after each addition until mixture clings together.
5. Form dough into ball; wrap in aluminum foil; refrigerate 30 minutes or longer.

Filling
1. Pare potatoes, carrot, onion using PARING KNIFE; coarsely chop using FRENCH CHEF'S KNIFE.
2. Cut meat in ½-inch cubes using PETITE CARVER.
3. In a 3-quart SAUCE PAN, cook potatoes, carrots, onions until tender; add salt.
4. Add meat cubes, gravy, raisins, cinnamon, cloves, oregano, pepper; heat 5 minutes.

5. Roll out pastry on floured board into two 13-inch squares; line bottom and sides of 9-inch square bake pan with pastry.
6. Pour filling into pan; arrange peach halves on top; cover with pastry; crimp edge of pastry.
7. Bake 30 minutes at 375° F.
8. Beat egg whites until soft peaks are formed; beat in sugar until meringue is stiff and glossy.
9. Spread meringue over top of pie; bake 3–5 minutes at 425° F. or until meringue is golden brown.
10. Cut in squares.
11. Eight–nine servings.

Hungarian Beef Strips

2 pounds of beef tenderloin
1 medium onion
4 large mushrooms
1 green pepper
1 red pepper
3 tablespoons vegetable oil
1¼ teaspoons paprika
½ teaspoon salt

1. Cut tenderloin in 3 x 1 x ¼-inch strips using PETITE CARVER.
2. Peel onion using PARING KNIFE; cut in thin slices using TRIMMER.
3. Chop mushrooms using FRENCH CHEF'S KNIFE.
4. Seed peppers; cut into thin strips using TRIMMER.
5. Heat 2 tablespoons oil in 10-inch FRY PAN over medium-high heat; brown beef strips well on both sides; remove from pan using PERFORATED SPOON.
6. Add 1 tablespoon oil; sauté onions 5–8 minutes stirring with TURNING FORK; remove from heat; stir in paprika.
7. Add browned meat, mushrooms, green pepper, red pepper, salt.
8. Heat until sizzling begins; reduce heat to low; cover; simmer 25–30 minutes.
9. Serve with hot buttered rice.
10. Four–five servings.

Entrees

Belgian Beef Casserole

3 pounds round steak
2 medium onions
6 tablespoons butter or margarine
½ cup instant-type flour
1½ cups hot water
1 cup light beer
2 teaspoons salt
⅛ teaspoon garlic powder
1 bay leaf
½ teaspoon sugar
⅛ teaspoon nutmeg
¼ teaspoon oregano
1½ teaspoons vinegar

1. Cut round steak in 1-inch cubes using PETITE CARVER.
2. Peel onions using PARING KNIFE; cut in thin slices using TRIMMER.
3. Melt 2 tablespoons butter in 10-inch FRY PAN over medium-high heat; brown meat cubes, stirring with TURNING FORK; transfer to 2-quart casserole using PERFORATED SPOON.
4. Melt remaining butter over medium heat; brown onions; transfer to casserole.
5. Stir in flour using MIX-STIR; cook 1 minute; gradually add water, beer, stirring constantly.
6. Add salt, garlic powder, bay leaf, sugar, nutmeg, oregano, vinegar; bring to a boil.
7. Pour gravy over meat, onions; cover; bake 2 hours at 325° F.
8. Serve with hot buttered noodles.
9. Five–six servings.

Flank Steak Bourbon

2 cups tomato sauce
¼ cup chopped chives
1 teaspoon seasoned salt
¼ teaspoon pepper
½ teaspoon celery salt
¼ cup bourbon
1 4-ounce can chopped mushrooms plus liquid
1 flank steak, 1-1¼ pounds

1. Combine tomato sauce, chives, seasoned salt, bourbon, mushrooms plus liquid; blend well using MIX-STIR.
2. Score flank steak on both sides with criss-cross cuts using PETITE CARVER; cover with Alcoa Wrap. (Do not press foil onto meat.)
3. Refrigerate about 12 hours; spoon marinade over beef several times using SOLID SPOON.
4. Bake uncovered 1½–2 hours at 325° F.; baste occasionally with marinade.
5. Four–five servings.

Beef Burgundy

1 garlic clove
1½ cups red wine
1 tablespoon pickling spice
3 pound bottom round beef, 1-inch thick
1 medium carrot
1 medium onion
1 stalk celery

1. Mince garlic clove using FRENCH CHEF'S KNIFE; add wine, pickling spices; blend well.
2. Place beef in shallow bake pan; pour marinade over beef; cover with Alcoa Wrap. (Do not press foil onto meat.)
3. Refrigerate about 12 hours; spoon marinade over beef several times using SOLID SPOON.
4. Scrape carrot, peel onion using PARING KNIFE; slice using TRIMMER.
5. Cut celery in ½-inch pieces using FRENCH CHEF'S KNIFE.
6. Strain marinade; pour over beef once again; add carrots, onions, celery.
7. Bake uncovered 2–2½ hours at 325° F.; baste occasionally with marinade.
8. Eight servings.

Beef Teriyaki (Japan)

2 pounds boneless sirloin,
  ¼-inch thick
¼ cup sherry wine
⅓ cup Japanese soy sauce
⅓ cup canned chicken broth
1 tablespoon sugar
2 teaspoons cornstarch
1 tablespoon cold water

1. Trim meat of excess fat using TRIMMER; cut into 12 pieces using BUTCHER KNIFE; pound meat slightly with edge of saucer or meat pounder.
2. To make Teriyaki Sauce: Blend together sherry, soy sauce, broth using MIX-STIR; reserve ¼ cup sauce.
3. Marinate meat in Teriyaki Sauce about 1 hour.
4. To make Teriyaki Glaze: Combine the reserved ¼ cup sauce, sugar in 1-quart SAUCE PAN heat but do not boil.
5. Dissolve cornstarch in water; stir into hot sauce using MIX-STIR; cook over medium heat until thick and clear; pour into bowl; set aside.
6. Broil meat for 1–2 minutes per side (medium or well done).
7. Cut meat into 1-inch wide strips using TRIMMER; arrange on platters of COMBO SERVERS; top with Teriyaki Glaze.
8. Six servings.
Variation: Boned chicken breasts, cut in half, may be substituted for beef; broil 4–5 minutes per side.

Flank Steak Teriyaki

1 clove garlic
4 green onions
½ cup vegetable oil
¼ cup soy sauce
¼ cup honey
2 tablespoons cider vinegar
2 tablespoons sherry wine
2 teaspoons ground ginger
2 pounds flank steak, not scored

1. Mince garlic, green onions using FRENCH CHEF'S KNIFE.
2. Press garlic against side of small bowl with back of wooden spoon.
3. Add onions, oil, soy sauce, honey, vinegar, sherry, ginger; beat until well blended using MIX-STIR.
4. Pour marinade over steak; cover; refrigerate at least six hours.
5. Place steak on broiler rack; broil 5–8 minutes per side.
6. To carve: Cut steak in thin slices with grain using PETITE CARVER; serve on COMBO SERVERS.
7. Six servings.

Delicious Meat Balls

2 pounds round steak, ground
1 pound pork tenderloin, ground
6 eggs, beaten
2 teaspoons salt
¼ teaspoon pepper
¼ cup all purpose flour
¼ cup salad oil or shortening
2 tablespoons all purpose flour
2 10½-ounce cans condensed beef
  consommé, undiluted
1 tablespoon bottled sauce for gravy
1 cup sherry wine

1. Combine beef, pork, eggs, salt, pepper, flour; toss together lightly using TURNING FORK.
2. Shape meat into balls, ¾ to 1-inch in diameter.
3. Heat oil in 10-inch FRY PAN.
4. Brown meat balls a few at a time in hot fat; remove with PERFORATED SPOON when browned.
5. When browning is complete, add the 2 tablespoons flour to fat in FRY PAN; stir until smooth using MIX-STIR.
6. Add consommé, bottled sauce; cook several minutes, stirring constantly using MIX-STIR.
7. Add sherry, meat balls; simmer 10 minutes over low heat.
8. Seven–eight servings as entrée: Serve over buttered noodles. Approximately 70 meat balls as hot hors d'oeuvres.

Entrees

Chuck Wagon Special

1 small baking potato
2 small onions
1 small carrot
1 stalk celery
¼ pound beef sirloin
2 tablespoons chili sauce
1 teaspoon quick-cooking tapioca
¼ teaspoon salt
⅛ teaspoon pepper

1. Peel potato, onions using PARING KNIFE; cut potato in half using TRIMMER.
2. Scrape carrot with PARING KNIFE; cut into quarters using FRENCH CHEF'S KNIFE.
3. Chop celery using FRENCH CHEF'S KNIFE.
4. Cut beef into 1-inch cubes using TRIMMER.
5. Combine chili sauce, tapioca; spread in center of double-thick square of Alcoa Wrap.
6. On sauce, arrange potato, onions, carrot, celery; top with meat cubes; sprinkle with salt, pepper.
7. Bring torn edges of foil over food; fold together tightly with double folds; make double fold on each end.
8. Place on baking sheet; bake 1 hour at 425° F.
9. Serve in opened package; idea fare for the patio supper.
10. One serving.

Spicy Beef Casserole

2½ pounds boneless rump
¼ cup flour
1 tablespoon sugar
1 teaspoon salt
½ teaspoon dry mustard
¼ teaspoon ground allspice
⅛ teaspoon pepper
1 8-ounce can tomato sauce
¼ cup Burgundy wine
½ cup canned beef broth
2 tablespoons vinegar
1½ tablespoons Worcestershire sauce

1. Cut beef in 2-inch cubes using BUTCHER KNIFE.

2. Combine flour, sugar, salt, mustard, allspice, pepper; coat meat.
3. Place meat in 2-quart casserole; sprinkle remaining flour mixture over meat.
4. Blend together tomato sauce, Burgundy, beef broth, vinegar, Worcestershire sauce using MIX-STIR; pour over meat; cover.
5. Bake 2½ hours at 325° F.
6. Serve with hot buttered noodles.
7. Five–six servings.

Swiss Steak

1½ pounds round steak, 1½ inches thick
3 large onions
2 tablespoons flour
1 teaspoon salt
⅛ teaspoon pepper
2 tablespoons shortening
1 cup hot water

1. Trim excess fat from meat; cut into serving size pieces using PETITE CARVER.
2. Peel onions using PARING KNIFE; slice using TRIMMER.
3. Combine flour, salt, pepper.
4. Coat meat with flour mixture; pound with edge of saucer.
5. Melt shortening in 10-inch FRY PAN; brown meat on both sides over medium heat.
6. Add water, onions; cover; cook over low heat about 2 hours or until meat is tender; add more water if necessary.
7. Four–six servings.

Variations:

1. Use 1½ cups canned tomatoes instead of water.
2. Substitute tomato sauce or vegetable juice for all or part of water.
3. Add 2 tablespoons ketchup, ½ teaspoon prepared mustard to water.
4. Add 1 green pepper, seeded and cut into rings.

70

Sukiyaki (Japan)

12 green onions
4 large mushrooms
2 leaves Chinese cabbage
1½ pounds boneless sirloin
1 cup fresh spinach leaves
2 tablespoons peanut oil
1 5-ounce can bamboo shoots, drained
½ cup canned bean sprouts
⅓ cup Japanese soy sauce
2 tablespoons sugar
½ cup canned chicken broth
2 tablespoons sherry wine

1. Slice green onions diagonally in 2-inch lengths using TRIMMER.
2. Cut mushrooms in thin slices using TRIMMER.
3. Slice cabbage diagonally using TRIMMER.
4. Cut sirloin in very thin 1 x 2-inch slices using PETITE CARVER.
5. Chop spinach using FRENCH CHEF'S KNIFE.
6. Heat oil in 10-inch FRY PAN over medium-high heat.
7. Add onions, mushrooms, cabbage, bamboo shoots, bean sprouts; sauté 2 minutes, stirring constantly using TURNING FORK.
8. Combine soy sauce, sugar, broth, sherry; blend well using MIX-STIR; pour over vegetables; simmer 8–10 minutes, stirring occasionally.
9. Add meat; bring liquid to boil; add spinach; simmer 3–5 minutes or until meat loses its red color.
10. Serve with steamed rice.
11. Four servings.

Note: Sukiyaki may be prepared at table in electric FRY PAN or in blazer pan of chafing dish. Arrange vegetables and meat attractively on platters of COMBO SERVERS; pour broth mixture into pitcher. Use chop sticks or two forks when adding vegetables and meat to FRY PAN.

Meat Loaf

3 slices white bread
1 small onion
½ small green pepper
2 eggs
1½ pounds ground beef
½ pound ground pork
2 tablespoons bottled horseradish
1 tablespoon salt
¼ cup milk
¼ cup ketchup
1 teaspoon dry mustard

1. Cut bread into small cubes using SLICER.
2. Peel onion using PARING KNIFE; finely chop using FRENCH CHEF'S KNIFE.
3. Finely chop green pepper using FRENCH CHEF'S KNIFE.
4. Beat eggs using MIX-STIR.
5. Add eggs to ground meats; blend lightly with TURNING FORK.
6. Add remaining ingredients; mix thoroughly but do not stir more than necessary as it tends to toughen loaf.
7. Shape into an oval loaf; place in shallow cake pan.
8. Bake 1 hour at 400° F.
9. Six–eight servings.

Variations:

1. Pack mixture into 9 x 5 x 3-inch loaf pan; bake as above. To remove from pan, drain off liquid; unmold on cake rack; then turn right side up on heated platter.
2. Spread top with ½ cup ketchup before baking.
3. Place ½ of meat mixture in loaf pan; make three depressions using a tablespoon; place a shelled hard cooked egg in each depression; add remaining meat.
4. Pack mixture into ring mold. To serve, fill center with mashed potatoes.

Entrees

Sloppy Joes

---

1 small onion
½ small green pepper
2 medium tomatoes
1 4-ounce can button mushrooms
2 tablespoons fat
½ pound ground beef
1 cup tomato juice
¼ teaspoon paprika
¼ teaspoon pepper
½ teaspoon salt
4 sandwich buns

1. Peel onion using PARING KNIFE; slice using TRIMMER.
2. Finely chop green pepper using FRENCH CHEF'S KNIFE.
3. Dip tomatoes into boiling water for about 1 minute using TURNING FORK; peel; core using PARING KNIFE; cut into eighths using TRIMMER.
4. Drain mushrooms; finely chop using FRENCH CHEF'S KNIFE.
5. Sauté onion, green pepper in fat in 10-inch FRY PAN until lightly browned, stirring with TURNING FORK.
6. Add tomatoes, mushrooms, beef, tomato juice, paprika, pepper, salt; cover.
7. Cook over low heat 15–20 minutes; thicken juice if desired.
8. Slice buns in half using SLICER; toast under broiler.
9. Serve over toasted buns.
10. Four servings.

Double Decker Hamburger

---

4 large stuffed olives
1 medium onion
1½ pounds ground round steak
¾ cup cold water
1 teaspoon salt
¼ teaspoon pepper
¼ cup ketchup
3 tablespoons soft butter or margarine

1. Slice olives using TRIMMER.
2. Peel onion using PARING KNIFE; slice using TRIMMER; separate into rings.
3. Combine meat, water, salt, pepper; shape into 8 flat patties.
4. Preheat 10-inch FRY PAN until drop of water dances on the surface; add meat patties; brown quickly on both sides.
5. Line shallow baking pan with Alcoa Wrap; place 4 patties in pan.
6. Spread ketchup over top of patties using SPREADER SPATULA; arrange olive slices over ketchup.
7. Top with remaining 4 patties; spread with butter using SPREADER SPATULA.
8. Insert toothpick through center of each patty; hang onion rings over toothpicks.
9. Bake 25–30 minutes at 375° F.
10. Four servings.

Chili Con Carne

---

1 small onion
1 tablespoon butter or margarine
1 pound ground beef
1 No. 2 can red kidney beans
1 10½-ounce can condensed tomato soup
1 teaspoon salt
¼ teaspoon chili powder

1. Peel onion using PARING KNIFE; finely chop using FRENCH CHEF'S KNIFE.
2. Melt butter in 10-inch FRY PAN; add onions, meat; cook until brown, stirring frequently with TURNING FORK.
3. Add kidney beans, tomato soup, salt, chili powder; stir; cover.
4. Cook over low heat 20–25 minutes; stir occasionally.
5. Four servings.

Corned Beef

4-5 pounds mild cure brisket of beef
3 medium onions
1 clove garlic
1 stalk celery
1 medium carrot
2 sprigs parsley
3 whole cloves
6 peppercorns
1 bay leaf

1. Wipe meat with damp cloth; place in ROUND ROASTER; cover with cold water.
2. Peel onions using PARING KNIFE; slice using TRIMMER.
3. Peel garlic clove; cut into quarters using PARING KNIFE.
4. Cut celery, carrot in 2-inch pieces using FRENCH CHEF'S KNIFE.
5. Snip parsley using KITCHEN SHEARS.
6. Add onions, garlic, celery, carrot, parsley, cloves, peppercorns, bay leaf to ROUND ROASTER; cover.
7. Bring to boil over medium-high heat; reduce to low; simmer 4–5 hours or until meat is tender; remove any scum that appears with the PERFORATED SPOON.
8. Remove from stock; slice with the SLICER; serve with horseradish sauce.

20th Century Wieners

3 tomatoes
2 medium onions
8 wieners
⅛ teaspoon basil
⅓ cup shredded sharp cheese

1. Core tomatoes using PARING KNIFE; slice using TRIMMER.
2. Peel onions using PARING knife; slice using TRIMMER.
3. Cut wieners in 1-inch pieces using TRIMMER.
4. Alternate tomatoes, onions, wieners in 10-inch FRY PAN; sprinkle basil on top.
5. Cover; cook over low heat 20–25 minutes.

6. Sprinkle cheese over top just before serving.
7. Four servings.

Corned Beef and Cabbage

1. Follow directions for Corned Beef.
2. Wash; quarter medium head cabbage using BUTCHER KNIFE; remove core.
3. About 20 minutes before corned beef is done, place cabbage wedges on top of meat.
4. Cover; boil until cabbage is just tender.

Calves Liver, German Style

4 medium red cooking apples
3 medium onions
1 pound calves liver
3 large sprigs parsley
3 tablespoons butter or margarine
Salt, pepper
3 tablespoons flour
1 tablespoon butter or margarine

1. Core apples using PARING KNIFE; cut in ¼-inch rings using TRIMMER.
2. Peel onions using PARING KNIFE; slice using TRIMMER; separate into rings.
3. Cut liver into ¼-inch slices using PETITE CARVER.
4. Snip parsley using KITCHEN SHEARS.
5. Melt butter in 10-inch FRY PAN; sauté apple rings until just tender; remove from pan using TURNER; keep warm in oven.
6. Sauté onion rings until transparent; remove from pan using TURNER; keep warm in oven.
7. Season liver with salt, pepper; coat with flour.
8. Melt remaining 1 tablespoon butter in FRY PAN; sauté liver until nicely browned, about 3–5 minutes per side.
9. Serve liver topped with apple rings, onion rings, snipped parsley.
10. Four servings.

Entrees

Exotic Greek Stew

3 pounds lean beef
2½ pounds small onions
1 tablespoon salt
⅓ cup butter or margarine, melted
1 6-ounce can tomato paste
⅓ cup red wine
2 tablespoons wine vinegar
1 tablespoon brown sugar
⅛ teaspoon garlic salt
1 bay leaf
1 small cinnamon stick
½ teaspoon whole cloves

1. Cut meat into 1½-inch cubes using PETITE CARVER.
2. Peel onions using PARING KNIFE.
3. Place meat, onions in ROUND ROASTER; sprinkle with salt; add melted butter. *(Do not brown meat.)*
4. Combine remaining ingredients; pour over meat; *do not stir.*
5. Cover; bake 5 hours at 250° F.; stir gently to blend meat and sauce before serving.
6. Six–eight servings.

5-Hour Stew

2 pounds lean chuck, lamb or veal
1 5¼-ounce can water chestnuts, drained
1 1-pound can tomatoes
1½ pound package frozen stew vegetables
1 tablespoon sugar
3 tablespoons quick cooking tapioca
1 tablespoon salt
¼ teaspoon pepper
¼ cup red wine

1. Cut meat into 1½-inch cubes using PETITE CARVER.
2. Slice water chestnuts with TRIMMER.

3. Combine all ingredients in a 3-quart casserole or ROUND ROASTER. *(Do not brown meat);* stir gently to blend.
4. Cover; bake 5 hours at 250° F.; stir gently before serving.
5. Five–six servings.

Braised Veal Chops (France)

4 loin veal chops, 1-inch thick
1 medium onion
1 carrot
1 stalk celery
3 large sprigs parsley
Salt, pepper
½ teaspoon basil
3 tablespoons vegetable oil
1 cup dry white wine
½ cup canned chicken broth
2 tablespoons butter or margarine
¾ cup fresh bread crumbs

1. Trim chops of excess fat using TRIMMER.
2. Peel onion using PARING KNIFE; chop onion, carrot, celery using FRENCH CHEF'S KNIFE.
3. Snip parsley using KITCHEN SHEARS.
4. Season chops with salt, pepper, basil.
5. Heat oil in 10-inch FRY PAN over medium-high heat; brown chops on both sides; remove using TURNING FORK.
6. Sauté onion, carrot, celery in oil 5 minutes; stir with TURNING FORK.
7. Add wine; boil several minutes or until liquid is reduced to ½ cup; add chicken broth.
8. In 8-inch FRY PAN, melt butter; stir in bread crumbs, parsley until thoroughly coated with butter.
9. Return chops to large FRY PAN; top with bread crumbs; cover; simmer 45 minutes.
10. Four servings.

Sesame Veal

1 pound veal steak
2 tablespoons flour
½ teaspoon salt
½ teaspoon poultry seasoning
½ teaspoon paprika
⅛ teaspoon pepper
2 tablespoons fat
½ cup soft bread crumbs
1 tablespoon butter or margarine, melted
¼ cup grated Parmesan cheese
2 tablespoons sesame seeds, toasted
½ cup hot water

1. Cut veal into serving pieces using PETITE CARVER.
2. Combine flour, salt, poultry seasoning, paprika, pepper; coat veal in flour mixture.
3. Melt fat in 10-inch FRY PAN; add veal; brown on all sides.
4. Place meat in shallow baking pan.
5. Combine bread crumbs, melted butter, Parmesan cheese, sesame seed; spoon over veal.
6. Pour water around veal.
7. Bake 45–50 minutes at 350° F.
8. Serve sauce from pan over veal.
9. Three–four servings.

Veal Cacciatora

1½ pounds veal round steak
1 medium onion
1 medium green pepper
2 large sprigs parsley
¼ cup olive oil
1 15-ounce can tomato sauce
⅓ cup white wine
1 teaspoon salt
¼ teaspoon pepper
¼ teaspoon instant minced garlic
1 teaspoon oregano
1 bay leaf

1. Cut veal steak into 2 x ½-inch strips using TRIMMER.
2. Peel onion using PARING KNIFE; slice using TRIMMER.
3. Seed green pepper; cut into thin strips using TRIMMER.
4. Snip parsley using KITCHEN SHEARS.
5. Heat oil in 10-inch FRY PAN; brown veal on both sides.
6. Add onion, green pepper; sauté 3 minutes.
7. Blend in remaining ingredients; cover; simmer 55–60 minutes.
8. Serve with hot buttered spaghetti or noodles.
9. Six servings.

Variation: Six serving pieces of chicken may be substituted for veal.

Wiener Schnitzel

1 pound veal cutlet, ½-inch thick
½ cup flour
1 teaspoon salt
2 eggs, beaten
1 cup crushed cornflakes
2 tablespoons butter or margarine
½ cup blanched, toasted almonds

1. Cut veal into serving pieces using PETITE CARVER.
2. Combine flour, salt; sprinkle half of flour mixture over veal; pound into meat using rim of saucer.
3. Turn meat; pound remaining flour into second side.
4. Dip meat into beaten egg, then into crushed cornflakes.
5. Melt butter in 10-inch FRY PAN; brown veal on both sides; cover; simmer until tender, about 30 minutes.
6. Sprinkle toasted almonds over each serving.
7. Three–four servings.

Fry Pan Kebabs

1 pound leg of lamb
2 green peppers
2 tomatoes
6 tablespoons wine vinegar
6 tablespoons water
¼ cup butter or margarine
½ teaspoon salt
¼ teaspoon pepper

1. Cut lamb in 1-inch cubes using TRIMMER.
2. Seed green peppers using TRIMMER; pour boiling water over peppers; let stand 5 minutes; drain; cut into 24 one-inch squares using FRENCH CHEF'S KNIFE.
3. Cut each tomato in eight wedges using TRIMMER.
4. Combine vinegar, water; pour over lamb; cover with aluminum foil; refrigerate 1 hour; turn meat once or twice.
5. Melt butter in 10-inch FRY PAN over medium heat; brown marinated lamb thoroughly on all sides about 15 minutes; stir with TURNING FORK; remove from pan using PERFORATED SPOON; cool slightly.
6. Arrange lamb, green pepper, tomato alternately on 8 short skewers; sprinkle with salt, pepper.
7. Place kebabs in FRY PAN; cover.
8. Cook 15 minutes, turning occasionally using TURNING FORK.
9. Eight servings.

Grecian Lamb Balls

1 small onion
1 medium eggplant
2 large sprigs parsley
1½ pounds ground lamb
1 teaspoon salt
⅛ teaspoon pepper
3 tablespoons vegetable oil
1 8-ounce can tomato sauce
2 tablespoons instant onion flakes
2 tablespoons vinegar
1 tablespoon brown sugar
¼ teaspoon salt
⅛ teaspoon pepper
⅛ teaspoon mustard
½ teaspoon cinnamon
¼ teaspoon ground cloves

1. Peel onion using PARING KNIFE; finely chop using FRENCH CHEF'S KNIFE.
2. Slice eggplant using PETITE CARVER; peel using PARING KNIFE; finely chop enough to make 2½ cups using FRENCH CHEF'S KNIFE.
3. Snip parsley using KITCHEN SHEARS.
4. Lightly toss together onion, eggplant, parsley, lamb, salt, pepper using TURNING FORK.
5. Shape into 20 balls using about ¼ cup mixture for each.
6. Heat oil in 10-inch FRY PAN over medium heat; brown meatballs on all sides; drain off excess fat.
7. Combine remaining ingredients; pour over meatballs.
8. Cover; simmer 45 minutes.
9. Four–five servings.

Entrees

County Kerry Pork Chops

4 pork chops, ½-inch thick
1 small onion
3 medium potatoes
1 pound cabbage
2 tablespoons vegetable oil
1 10½-ounce can condensed cream
of celery soup
½ cup milk
¼ cup flour
1½ teaspoons salt
⅛ teaspoon pepper

1. Trim excess fat from chops using TRIMMER.
2. Peel onion using PARING KNIFE; dice using FRENCH CHEF'S KNIFE.
3. Pare potatoes using PARING KNIFE; cut in thin slices using FRENCH CHEF'S KNIFE.
4. Cut cabbage in wedges using BUTCHER KNIFE; shred using SLICER.
5. Heat oil in 10-inch FRY PAN over medium-high heat; quickly brown chops; remove using TURNING FORK.
6. Add onion, soup, milk to FRY PAN; blend; set aside.
7. Starting with potatoes, put alternate layers of potatoes, cabbage into a 2-quart casserole; sprinkle each layer with mixture of flour, salt, pepper; pour soup mixture over each layer.
8. Place chops on top; cover; bake 1¼ hours at 350° F.
9. Four servings.

Pork Chops Pierre

1 small onion
2 stalks celery
1 large onion
1 large green pepper
1 tablespoon butter or margarine
¼ cup water
½ cup ketchup
2 tablespoons vinegar

1 tablespoon lemon juice
1 tablespoon Worcestershire sauce
1 tablespoon brown sugar
½ teaspoon salt
⅛ teaspoon pepper
8 loin pork chops, ½-inch thick

1. Peel small onion using PARING KNIFE; finely chop onion, celery using FRENCH CHEF'S KNIFE.
2. Peel large onion using PARING KNIFE; thinly slice using PETITE CARVER.
3. Seed green pepper; cut into rings using TRIMMER.
4. Combine butter, onion, celery in 2-quart SAUCE PAN; sauté until tender.
5. Add water, ketchup, vinegar, lemon juice, Worcestershire sauce, sugar, salt, pepper; cover; simmer 20 minutes.
6. Brown chops on both sides in preheated 10-inch FRY PAN.
7. Place chops in 9 x 13-inch bake pan; pour sauce over chops; top with onion slices; pepper rings.
8. Cover pan with Alcoa Wrap; bake 45–50 minutes at 400° F.
9. Eight servings.

Maggie's Lamb Chops

4 loin lamb chops, 1-inch thick
Salt, pepper
4 slices American cheese
4 slices Bermuda onion
8 tablespoons dairy sour cream

1. Trim chops of excess fat using TRIMMER; secure tails to thickest part of chops with toothpicks.
2. Sprinkle with salt, pepper.
3. Place chops in shallow baking pan.
4. Place 1 slice cheese, 1 slice onion on each chop.
5. Put 2 tablespoons sour cream on each chop.
6. Add no water; do not cover.
7. Bake 1 hour at 375° F.
8. Four servings.

77

Entrees

Glazed Ham Balls

1 small onion
1 pound ground ham
1 pound ground pork
⅔ cup cracker crumbs
2 eggs, beaten
1¼ cups evaporated milk
¼ teaspoon salt
¼ teaspoon thyme
1 cup brown sugar, firmly packed
1 teaspoon dry mustard
3 tablespoons vinegar

1. Peel onion using PARING KNIFE; finely chop using FRENCH CHEF'S KNIFE.
2. Combine ham, pork, cracker crumbs, eggs, evaporated milk, salt, thyme, onion; toss together lightly using TURNING FORK.
3. Make 16 balls (using #16 ice cream scoop); place balls in 9 x 13-inch bake pan.
4. Combine brown sugar, mustard, vinegar in 1-quart SAUCE PAN; bring to boil over medium heat; pour over ham balls.
5. Bake uncovered 1 hour at 350° F.
6. Eight servings.

Pork Chops Alexander

1 cup dried apricots
2 cups warm water
½ cup flour
½ teaspoon salt
¼ teaspoon pepper
¼ teaspoon thyme
6 loin pork chops, ¾-inch thick
2 tablespoons oil
¼ cup maple syrup

1. Combine apricots, water in 1-quart SAUCE PAN; cook until tender; drain.
2. Combine flour, salt, pepper, thyme; dust over both sides of chops.
3. Heat oil in 10-inch FRY PAN; brown chops on both sides.
4. Combine apricots, syrup; pour over chops.
5. Cover; cook 1 hour over low heat until chops are tender.
6. Six servings.

Hawaiian Ribs

4 pounds spareribs
2 green peppers
¾ cup cornstarch
¼ cup molasses
¼ cup soy sauce
½ cup sugar
¾ cup vinegar
¾ cup water
¾ cup pineapple juice
1 cup pineapple chunks

1. Cut spareribs into 1½-inch strips using BUTCHER KNIFE.
2. Seed green peppers; cut into 1-inch cubes using TRIMMER.
3. Brown ribs in ROUND ROASTER; remove from pan.
4. Combine cornstarch, molasses, soy sauce to make paste.
5. Spread paste on both sides of ribs using SPREADER SPATULA.
6. Rebrown quickly in ROUND ROASTER.
7. Combine sugar, vinegar, water, pineapple juice in 1-quart SAUCE PAN; heat until sugar dissolves; pour over ribs.
8. Cover; simmer 25–30 minutes.
9. Add pineapple chunks, green pepper cubes; simmer additional 5 minutes.
10. Four–five servings.

Entrees

Spaghetti Carbonara (Italy)

1 clove garlic
8 large sprigs parsley
8 ounces uncooked spaghetti
2 tablespoons butter or margarine
2 cups diced cooked ham
3 eggs
½ cup grated Parmesan cheese

1. Mince garlic using FRENCH CHEF'S KNIFE.
2. Snip parsley using KITCHEN SHEARS.
3. Cook spaghetti in 4-quart SAUCE PAN following package directions; drain; return to pan.
4. Melt butter in 8-inch FRY PAN; sauté garlic, ham 3–4 minutes over medium heat, stirring with TURNING FORK.
5. Beat eggs using MIX-STIR; add cheese, parsley; pour over hot drained spaghetti; add ham; toss quickly with two forks until all strands are coated.
6. Four–six servings.

Lasagne (Italy)

1 small onion
2 small sprigs parsley
1 pound ground beef
2 cups canned tomatoes
1 15-ounce can tomatoe sauce
⅛ teaspoon instant minced garlic
1 teaspoon oregano
1 teaspoon salt
½ pound lasagne noodles
¾ pound Mozzarella cheese, grated
6 ounces Cheddar cheese, grated
4 ounces Parmesan cheese, grated

1. Peel onion using PARING KNIFE; chop using FRENCH CHEF'S KNIFE.
2. Snip parsley using KITCHEN SHEARS.
3. Preheat 10-inch FRY PAN until drop of water dances on the surface; add beef; brown thoroughly using TURNING FORK to stir.
4. Add onion, parsley, tomatoes, tomato sauce, garlic, oregano, salt; cover; simmer 1 hour.
5. Cook noodles in 4-quart SAUCE PAN according to package directions; drain.
6. Cover bottom of 9 x 13-inch bake pan with sauce; add a layer of noodles.
7. Sprinkle with ½ the Mozzarella cheese, then more sauce; repeat layers.
8. Top with Cheddar, Parmesan cheese.
9. Bake 30 minutes at 350° F.
10. Let stand 5 minutes for easier cutting; remove serving pieces with TURNER.
11. Twelve servings.

Egg Foo Yung (China)

¼ pound cooked chicken
¼ pound cooked shrimp
4 mushrooms
8 green onions
1 stalk celery
5 eggs
½ teaspoon salt
½ cup bean sprouts
3-4 tablespoons peanut oil

1. Coarsely chop chicken, shrimp, mushrooms using FRENCH CHEF'S KNIFE.
2. Mince green onions, celery using FRENCH CHEF'S KNIFE.
3. Beat eggs using MIX-STIR; blend in salt.
4. Stir in chicken, shrimp, mushrooms, onions, celery, bean sprouts.
5. Heat ½ tablespoon oil in 8-inch FRY PAN over medium-high heat; reduce heat to medium.
6. Pour ¼ cup egg mixture into FRY PAN; cook 1 minute on each side (should be lightly browned); keep warm in 200° F. oven; repeat until all batter is used; add more oil as needed.
7. Serve with Foo Yung Sauce.
8. Four servings.

79

Entrees

Onion Quiche (Switzerland)

2 medium onions
2 hard cooked eggs
Pastry for one crust
2 tablespoons butter or margarine
¼ pound Swiss cheese, grated
4 eggs
1 cup whipping cream
½ cup milk
¾ teaspoon salt
⅛ teaspoon nutmeg
⅛ teaspoon pepper

1. Peel onion using PARING KNIFE; slice in thin rings using TRIMMER.
2. Slice hard cooked eggs using TRIMMER.
3. Line Quiche Lorraine pan or 9-inch pie pan with pastry; trim and flute at top edge.
4. Prick well with TURNING FORK; bake 10–15 minutes at 425° F. until pastry just begins to brown; cool.
5. Melt butter in 10-inch FRY PAN over medium-high heat; sauté onions until tender but not brown, stirring with TURNING FORK.
6. Sprinkle ½ the grated cheese over bottom of pastry shell; arrange onions over cheese; sprinkle with remaining cheese.
7. Beat eggs thoroughly using MIX-STIR in medium sized bowl; blend in cream, milk, salt, nutmeg, pepper; pour over cheese, onion.
8. Arrange sliced eggs on top; push to submerge slices slightly.
9. Bake 15 minutes at 425° F., then reduce temperature to 300° F. for 30 minutes or until golden brown, custard set.
10. Seven–eight servings.

Maggie's Chicken Mornay

3 whole chicken breasts
½ cup flour
1 teaspoon salt
⅛ teaspoon pepper
⅛ teaspoon ginger
½ cup butter or margarine
1 cup water
Sauce
¼ cup butter or margarine
¼ cup flour
1 teaspoon salt
½ cup light cream
½ cup milk
1 cup grated American cheese
1 4-ounce can diced mushrooms, drained

1. Split chicken breasts in half using BUTCHER KNIFE and KITCHEN SHEARS.
2. Coat chicken breasts with combined flour, salt, pepper, ginger mixture.
3. Melt butter in 10-inch FRY PAN; brown chicken breasts on both sides; cover; cook over low heat 30–45 minutes or until tender.
4. Transfer chicken breasts to 9 x 13-inch bake pan.
5. Add water to drippings in FRY PAN; stir with MIX-STIR to loosen any sediment; set aside.
6. Melt butter in 2-quart SAUCE PAN; blend in flour, salt with MIX-STIR.
7. Gradually add cream, milk, reserved liquid from FRY PAN; cook over low heat until thickened, stirring constantly with MIX-STIR.
8. Add ½ cup cheese, mushrooms; blend well.
9. Pour sauce over chicken; sprinkle with remaining cheese; bake 25–30 minutes at 350° F. until just lightly browned.
10. Six servings.

Chicken Fricassee (France)

1 medium onion
1 stalk celery
1 carrot
6 medium mushrooms
3 pound frying chicken, cut up
¼ cup flour
½ teaspoon salt
⅛ teaspoon white pepper
¼ cup butter or margarine
1 14-ounce can chicken broth
1 cup dry white wine
½ cup whipping cream
Salt, pepper

1. Peel onion using PARING KNIFE; cut in thin slices using TRIMMER.
2. Slice celery diagonally using TRIMMER.
3. Slice carrot thinly using FRENCH CHEF'S KNIFE.
4. Slice mushrooms using TRIM-MER.
5. Coat chicken with mixture of flour, salt, pepper; reserving any remaining flour.
6. Melt 3 tablespoons butter in 10-inch FRY PAN over medium heat; quickly fry chicken on all sides, turning frequently with TURNING FORK; do *not* brown; remove.
7. Add 1 tablespoon butter to FRY PAN; sauté onion, celery, carrot, mushrooms 5 minutes, stirring with TURNING FORK.
8. Blend in any remaining flour mixture; slowly stir in broth, wine using MIX-STIR.
9. Add chicken; bring to a boil; cover; simmer 25–30 minutes or until chicken is tender.
10. Remove chicken; boil liquid until reduced to 2 cups.
11. Gradually stir in cream using MIX-STIR; season with salt, pepper to taste.
12. Return chicken to sauce; heat.
13. Six servings.

Belgium Baked Codfish

2 pounds codfish fillets
Salt, pepper
2 medium onions
½ cup dry white wine
2 tablespoons dry bread crumbs
3 tablespoons grated Cheddar cheese
1 teaspoon paprika
¼ cup butter or margarine
2 parsley sprigs

1. Place fillets in 9 x 13-inch bake pan; season with salt, pepper.
2. Peel onions using PARING KNIFE; cut in thin slices using TRIMMER.
3. Lay onion slices over fillets; pour wine around fillets.
4. Combine bread crumbs, cheese, paprika; sprinkle over fillets; dot with butter.
5. Snip parsley using KITCHEN SHEARS; sprinkle over top.
6. Bake 25 minutes at 350° F.
7. Six servings.

Baked Salmon with Herb Butter

1 small onion
1 clove garlic
2 sprigs parsley
2 pounds salmon fillets
¼ cup butter or margarine, softened
3 tablespoons lemon juice
½ teaspoon basil
1 teaspoon salt
½ teaspoon pepper

1. Peel onion using PARING KNIFE; finely chop using FRENCH CHEF'S KNIFE.
2. Mince garlic, parsley using FRENCH CHEF'S KNIFE.
3. Place salmon fillets in 9 x 13-inch bake pan.
4. Combine onion, garlic, parsley, butter, lemon juice, basil, salt, pepper; blend well using TURNING FORK.
5. Spread over salmon using SPREADER SPATULA.
6. Bake 25–30 minutes at 300° F. or until fish flakes.
7. Six–eight servings.

Entrees

Mexican Braised Duck

4-5 pound duck
¼ cup lemon juice
½ teaspoon salt
⅛ teaspoon pepper
2 tablespoons olive oil
2 12-ounce cans light beer
1 cup raw rice
1 cup frozen green peas, thawed
½ teaspoon salt
   Pepper
½ teaspoon ground coriander
2 sprigs parsley

1. Cut duck into serving pieces using BUTCHER KNIFE, KITCHEN SHEARS; trim off all fat using TRIMMER.
2. Brush duck with lemon juice; season with salt, pepper; cover; let stand 3 hours.
3. Heat olive oil in 10-inch FRY PAN over medium-high heat; brown duck well on both sides; pour off fat.
4. Add beer to FRY PAN; cover; simmer 45 minutes.
5. Remove duck; keep warm in 200° F. oven.
6. Skim fat from broth; measure 2 cups broth (add water, if necessary).
7. Combine broth, rice in FRY PAN; bring to a boil.
8. Add peas, salt, pepper, coriander; cover; simmer about 15 minutes or until all liquid has been absorbed.
9. Snip parsley with KITCHEN SHEARS; stir into rice; place in serving dish; top with duck.
10. Four–five servings.

Phillipine Red Snapper

1 large onion
½ green pepper
3 stalks celery
1 carrot
2 pounds red snapper fillets
2 tablespoons lemon juice
½ teaspoon salt
2 tablespoons olive oil
1 1-pound can tomatoes
2 tablespoons ketchup
½ teaspoon salt
⅛ teaspoon pepper

1. Peel onion using PARING KNIFE; finely chop using FRENCH CHEF'S KNIFE.
2. Seed green pepper using TRIMMER; chop using FRENCH CHEF'S KNIFE.
3. Chop celery, carrot using FRENCH CHEF'S KNIFE.
4. Place fish fillets on large plate; sprinkle with lemon juice; let stand 30 minutes; place fillets in 9 x 13-inch bake pan, discarding excess lemon juice.
5. Heat olive oil in 10-inch FRY PAN over medium-high heat; sauté onion, green pepper, celery, carrot 5 minutes, stirring with TURNING FORK.
6. Add tomatoes, ketchup, salt, pepper; cover; simmer 30 minutes.
7. Pour vegetable mixture over fillets; bake 35 minutes at 400° F.
8. Six servings.

Mexican Style Perch

1 small onion
¼ green pepper
1 canned pimiento
¼ cup soft butter or margarine
1 teaspoon salt
¾ teaspoon chili powder
⅛ teaspoon thyme
⅛ teaspoon pepper
3 tablespoons dry bread crumbs
1½ pounds perch fillets

1. Peel onion using PARING KNIFE; mince using FRENCH CHEF'S KNIFE.
2. Seed green pepper using TRIMMER; mince using FRENCH CHEF'S KNIFE.
3. Mince pimiento using FRENCH CHEF'S KNIFE.
4. Combine onion, green pepper, pimiento, butter, salt, chili powder, thyme, pepper, bread crumbs; blend well using TURNING FORK.
5. Place fillets side by side in 9 x 13-inch bake pan; spread butter mixture over fillets using SPREADER SPATULA.
6. Bake 25–30 minutes at 425° F.
7. Six servings.

Salmon Casserole

2 tablespoons instant minced onion
¼ cup cold water
3 cups cooked rice
1 pound can salmon, drained, flaked
2 teaspoons salt
¼ teaspoon pepper
1 whole egg
2 egg whites
2 tablespoons butter or margarine, melted

1. Combine onion, water; let stand 5 minutes.
2. Combine onion, rice, salmon, salt, pepper; toss together lightly with TURNING FORK.

3. Beat egg, egg whites with MIX-STIR; add to salmon mixture; blend together.
4. Press into greased 1½-quart casserole; brush top with melted butter.
5. Bake 30 minutes at 375° F.
6. Garnish with lemon wedges, parsley; serve with Lemon Cucumber Sauce.
7. Four–five servings.

Halibut Supreme

1½ pounds halibut fillets
1 cup water
¼ cup dry white wine
¼ cup lemon juice
2 tablespoons butter or margarine
2 tablespoons flour
1 cup milk
¼ teaspoon salt
⅛ teaspoon pepper
¼ teaspoon onion salt
2 cups chopped, cooked spinach
¾ cup grated sharp cheese
2 eggs
1 tablespoon butter or margarine

1. Place fish in 10-inch FRY PAN; add water, wine, lemon juice; cover; simmer 5 minutes.
2. Remove fish using TURNER; place in 2-quart casserole.
3. Boil liquid until ¾ cup broth remains.
4. Melt butter in 2-quart SAUCE PAN; stir in flour using MIX-STIR; gradually add milk; cook, stirring constantly until thickened.
5. Add salt, pepper, onion salt, spinach, ¼ cup cheese; cook 5 minutes.
6. Beat eggs with MIX-STIR; stir into sauce.
7. Pour sauce over fish; sprinkle top with remaining cheese; dot with butter.
8. Bake 10–12 minutes at 400° F. until bubbly, cheese melts.
9. Six servings.

Vegetables

Stuffed Zucchini Boats

2 medium zucchini
2 hard cooked eggs
1 small stalk celery
2 green onions
1 tablespoon butter or margarine
1 tablespoon flour
½ cup milk
1 4½-ounce can deviled ham
1 teaspoon chopped parsley
1 teaspoon chopped chives
1 teaspoon salt
¼ teaspoon pepper
¼ teaspoon nutmeg
¾ cup whole wheat cracker crumbs

1. Slice zucchini in half lengthwise using BUTCHER KNIFE; scoop out centers, reserving pulp.
2. Chop eggs, celery using FRENCH CHEF'S KNIFE.
3. Mince green onions using FRENCH CHEF'S KNIFE.
4. Place zucchini pulp in 1-quart SAUCE PAN; cover with cold water; bring to a boil; simmer 5 minutes; drain.
5. Melt butter in 2-quart SAUCE PAN; stir in flour using MIX-STIR; add milk; cook until thick, smooth, stirring constantly.
6. Add zucchini pulp, eggs, celery, onions, deviled ham, parsley, chives, salt, pepper, nutmeg, ½ cup crumbs; blend thoroughly using TURNING FORK.
7. Fill each zucchini shell with stuffing; sprinkle with remaining crumbs; place in 9 x 13-inch bake pan.
8. Bake 30 minutes at 375° F.
9. Four servings.

Summer Vegetable Medley

2 cloves garlic
3 medium potatoes
4 carrots
2 onions
2 green peppers
1 small eggplant
2 zucchini
2 summer squash
¼ cup butter or margarine
1 8-ounce can tomato sauce
1 cup water
Dash Tabasco sauce
Salt, pepper

1. Cut garlic cloves in half using PARING KNIFE.
2. Pare potatoes using PARING KNIFE; cut in cubes using FRENCH CHEF'S KNIFE.
3. Scrape carrots using PARING KNIFE; cut in thin crosswise slices using FRENCH CHEF'S KNIFE.
4. Peel onions using PARING KNIFE; cut in thin slices using TRIMMER.
5. Seed green peppers; cut in eighths using TRIMMER.
6. Cut eggplant in cubes (do *not* pare) using FRENCH CHEF'S KNIFE.
7. Cut zucchini, summer squash, in thin slices using FRENCH CHEF'S KNIFE.
8. Sauté garlic in butter in 10-inch FRY PAN stirring with TURNING FORK; remove pieces.
9. Add vegetables, tomato sauce, water, Tabasco; cover; simmer 20–25 minutes, or until vegetables are tender.
10. Season with salt, pepper.
11. Eight servings.

Vegetables

Eggplant-Tomato Casserole

2 medium eggplants
1 teaspoon salt
2 tablespoons flour
2 1-pound cans stewed tomatoes
1 tablespoon instant chopped onion
2 teaspoons sugar
½ teaspoon paprika
¼ teaspoon oregano
⅛ teaspoon pepper
½ cup olive oil
½ cup grated Parmesan cheese

1. Slice eggplants in ¼-inch slices using PETITE CARVER; pare using PARING KNIFE; sprinkle with salt.
2. Blend flour, liquid from tomatoes together in 2-quart SAUCE PAN using MIX-STIR.
3. Add tomatoes, onion, sugar, paprika, oregano, pepper; bring to boil; simmer 5 minutes.
4. Heat 2 tablespoons olive oil in 10-inch FRY PAN over medium heat; fry eggplant slices until lightly browned, tender; drain on paper toweling; continue until all slices have been browned, adding more oil as necessary.
5. Line bottom of 9 x 13-inch bake pan with eggplant slices; top with half the tomato sauce; repeat layers; sprinkle cheese over top.
6. Bake 30 minutes at 350° F.
7. Six–eight servings.

Corn Curry (New Zealand)

3 tablespoons butter or margarine
2 tablespoons chopped green pepper
1 tablespoon instant minced onion
1 10-ounce package frozen corn
½ teaspoon salt
½ teaspoon curry powder
Dash pepper
½ cup dairy sour cream

1. Melt butter in 8-inch FRY PAN; sauté green pepper, onion about 1 minute over medium heat, stirring with TURNING FORK.
2. Add corn, salt, curry powder, pepper; cover; simmer 8–10 minutes or until corn is tender.
3. Stir in sour cream; heat, stirring constantly.
4. Four servings.

Cucumber Au Gratin (Ireland)

2 cucumbers
2 tomatoes
Salt, pepper
3 tablespoons butter or margarine
3 tablespoons flour
¼ teaspoon salt
1 cup milk
½ cup grated Cheddar cheese
2 tablespoons grated Cheddar cheese

1. Pare cucumbers using PARING KNIFE; cut in thin slices using TRIMMER.
2. Cut tomatoes in ¼-inch slices using TRIMMER.
3. Cook cucumber slices in boiling, salted water about 10 minutes; drain.
4. Arrange in shallow baking dish; sprinkle lightly with salt, pepper.
5. In a 1-quart SAUCE PAN, melt butter over low heat; stir in flour, salt using MIX-STIR, gradually stir in milk.
6. Cook over low heat, stirring constantly until thickened; add ½ cup grated cheese; stir until cheese melts.
7. Pour sauce over cucumbers; top with tomato slices, grated cheese.
8. Bake 10–15 minutes at 400° F. or until lightly browned.
9. Five–six servings.

Chinese Green Beans

1 pound fresh green beans
3 tablespoons peanut oil
1 4-ounce can sliced mushrooms,
   drained
1 teaspoon salt
1 teaspoon sugar
⅓ cup canned chicken broth
1 teaspoon cornstarch
1 tablespoon chicken broth

1. Remove ends from beans using PARING KNIFE; cut diagonally in 2-inch pieces using FRENCH CHEF'S KNIFE.
2. Heat oil in 10-inch FRY PAN over medium-high heat; add beans; fry 3–4 minutes, stirring constantly using TURNING FORK.
3. Add mushrooms, salt, sugar, chicken broth; blend together.
4. Cover; cook over medium heat 5 minutes until beans are tender but crisp.
5. Dissolve cornstarch in chicken broth; stir into beans; cook until thickened, stirring constantly.
6. Four–five servings.

Spanish Green Peas

2 whole canned pimientos
¼ cup ripe olives
2 tablespoons butter or margarine
½ teaspoon onion salt
¼ teaspoon crushed oregano
¼ teaspoon pepper
1 1-pound can green peas, drained

1. Chop pimientos using FRENCH CHEF'S KNIFE.
2. Slice olives using TRIMMER.
3. Melt butter in 1-quart SAUCE PAN; add onion salt, oregano, pepper; simmer 3 minutes.
4. Add peas, pimientos, olives; toss lightly to mix using TURNING FORK; cover; simmer 10 minutes or until peas are hot; shake pan occasionally.
5. Four servings.

French Green Peas

3 slices bacon
2 small onions
2 sprigs parsley
½ canned pimiento
3 tablespoons flour
1½ cups canned chicken broth
½ teaspoon salt
   Dash pepper
1 10-ounce package frozen peas

1. Dice bacon using TRIMMER.
2. Peel onions using PARING KNIFE; slice using TRIMMER.
3. Snip parsley using KITCHEN SHEARS.
4. Cut pimiento into strips using TRIMMER.
5. Fry bacon until crisp in 8-inch FRY PAN over medium heat; remove using PERFORATED SPOON; drain on paper toweling.
6. Add flour to bacon fat in pan; blend until smooth using MIX-STIR; cook over low heat 1–2 minutes.
7. Add chicken broth, salt, pepper; cook over medium heat, stirring constantly, until smooth, thickened.
8. Add peas, onions, parsley; cover; cook over low heat until peas are tender, about 20 minutes.
9. Garnish with crisp bacon, pimiento strips.
10. Four servings.

Vegetables

Mushrooms Baked in Foil

1 pint fresh mushrooms
Salt, pepper

1. Trim stems of mushrooms, remove blemishes using PARING KNIFE; wash; drain; dry.
2. Place mushrooms on double thick sheet of Alcoa Wrap; add salt, pepper.
3. Place sheet of Alcoa Wrap over mushrooms; fold each side over in double fold; seal tightly.
4. Place foil package on baking sheet; bake 30 minutes at 350° F.
5. Three–four servings.

Baked Stuffed Onions

6 large onions
¾ cup seasoned bread stuffing
¾ cup chopped cooked chicken
¾ cup thin white sauce
1 egg yolk
Salt, pepper
½ cup buttered cracker crumbs

1. Peel onions using PARING KNIFE; boil 10 minutes in salted water; drain; turn upside down to cool.
2. Remove centers of onions, leaving shell thick enough to retain shape.
3. Chop onion centers using FRENCH CHEF'S KNIFE; combine with stuffing, chicken, white sauce, egg yolk, salt, pepper using TURNING FORK.
4. Place each onion in center of square of Alcoa Wrap; bring sides of foil up around onion to form cup.
5. Fill onions with stuffing mixture; sprinkle cracker crumbs on top; place foil cups on baking sheet.
6. Bake 40 minutes at 350° F.
7. Serve in foil cups.
8. Six servings.

Souffléed Cauliflower

2 10-ounce packages frozen cauliflower
2 eggs, separated
1 10½-ounce can condensed mushroom soup, undiluted
2 tablespoons sherry wine
1 tablespoon light cream
¼ teaspoon salt
⅛ teaspoon pepper
½ cup grated Cheddar cheese
Paprika

1. Cook cauliflower as directed on package; drain; arrange in 1½-quart casserole.
2. Beat egg yolks slightly using MIX-STIR; add mushroom soup, sherry, cream, salt, pepper; beat thoroughly; add cheese.
3. Beat egg whites until stiff; fold into egg yolk mixture.
4. Pour over cauliflower; sprinkle with paprika.
5. Bake 20 minutes at 425° F.
6. Five–six servings.

Stuffed Artichokes with Mornay Sauce

4 artichokes
1 10-ounce package frozen cut asparagus
3 tablespoons butter or margarine
3 tablespoons flour
½ teaspoon salt
½ cup light cream
½ cup grated American cheese

1. Wash artichokes; drain; remove loose discolored leaves around base using PARING KNIFE.
2. Drop artichokes into boiling unsalted water to cover; simmer 15–20 minutes or until just tender. (Retain 1 cup liquid for sauce.)
3. Cut away fuzzy centers or "chokes" of artichokes using PARING KNIFE; discard; set artichokes aside.
4. Cook asparagus according to directions on package.
5. To make Mornay Sauce: Melt butter in 1-quart SAUCE PAN; add flour, salt, stirring with MIX-STIR.
6. Gradually add cream, the 1 cup artichoke liquid; cook over low heat, stirring constantly with MIX-STIR until thickened.
7. Add cheese; stir until melted.
8. Place each artichoke in center of sheet of Alcoa Wrap; crush foil around artichokes to form cups.
9. Fill centers of artichokes with asparagus; pour Mornay Sauce over top.
10. Place foil cups on baking sheet; bake 25–30 minutes at 350° F. or until sauce is bubbly, lightly browned.
11. Serve in foil cups.
12. Four servings.

Deviled Mushrooms

1 pint fresh mushrooms
Salt, pepper
2 teaspoons lemon juice
1 hard cooked egg yolk
1 raw egg yolk
½ cup dry bread crumbs
1 tablespoon butter or margarine, softened
Dash Tabasco sauce

1. Wash mushrooms; remove stems using PARING KNIFE.
2. Place mushroom caps and stems in 1-quart casserole; season with salt, pepper, lemon juice.
3. Mash hard cooked egg yolk using TURNING FORK; add raw yolk, bread crumbs, butter, Tabasco; blend thoroughly.
4. Sprinkle egg-bread crumb mixture over top of mushrooms.
5. Bake 20–25 minutes at 350° F.
6. Four servings.

Carrots in Sauce

1 pound carrots
4 whole cloves
1 bay leaf
2 tablespoons butter or margarine
2 tablespoons flour
1 cup milk
1 teaspoon chopped parsley
½ teaspoon salt
Dash cayenne pepper

1. Wash carrots; scrape using PARING KNIFE; dice using FRENCH CHEF'S KNIFE.
2. Put in 2-quart SAUCE PAN along with cloves, bay leaf; cover with boiling water; cover pan; simmer until tender.
3. Drain, reserving 1 cup water; set carrots aside.
4. Melt butter in SAUCE PAN; add flour, blending with MIX-STIR.
5. Add milk, reserved liquid; cook until thickened.
6. Add parsley, salt, cayenne, carrots; heat about 5 minutes.
7. Garnish with lemon slices if desired.
8. Six servings.

Vegetables

Baked Asparagus with Basil Sour Cream

¾ pound fresh asparagus spears
½ cup dairy sour cream
½ cup butter or margarine, melted
2 cups soft bread crumbs
1 teaspoon sweet basil
½ teaspoon salt

1. Wash asparagus; trim ends using FRENCH CHEF'S KNIFE.
2. Cook asparagus spears until just tender; place spears in 9-inch square bake pan; spread sour cream over spears using SPREADER SPATULA.
3. Combine melted butter, bread crumbs, basil, salt; toss together using TURNING FORK; sprinkle over sour cream.
4. Bake 15–20 minutes at 375° F. or until crumb topping is browned.
5. Three–four servings.

Golden Potato Wedges

2 medium baking potatoes
¼ cup butter or margarine, melted
½ cup fine dry bread crumbs
Salt, pepper
2 tablespoons butter or margarine

1. Pare potatoes using PARING KNIFE; cut potatoes in half crosswise using FRENCH CHEF'S KNIFE; cut each half in four long wedges.
2. Dip wedges in melted butter, then into bread crumbs; place in greased shallow baking dish; sprinkle with salt, pepper; dot with butter.
3. Bake 35–40 minutes at 400° F. or until tender, golden brown.
4. Two–three servings.

Corn Pudding

1 large green pepper
1 medium onion
4 slices white bread
¼ cup butter or margarine
¼ cup flour
2 teaspoons salt
1 teaspoon paprika
1 teaspoon dry mustard
⅛ teaspoon cayenne pepper
1 cup milk
2 eggs
2 No. 303 cans cream-style corn
3 tablespoons butter or margarine

1. Seed green pepper using PARING KNIFE; finely chop using FRENCH CHEF'S KNIFE.
2. Peel onion using PARING KNIFE; finely chop using FRENCH CHEF'S KNIFE.
3. Cut bread slices into cubes using FRENCH CHEF'S KNIFE.
4. Melt butter in 10-inch FRY PAN; sauté green pepper, onion 5 minutes using TURNING FORK to stir.
5. Add flour, salt, paprika, dry mustard, cayenne; blend using MIX-STIR.
6. Add milk; cook stirring constantly until thickened.
7. Beat eggs using MIX-STIR; add to sauce along with corn; blend well.
8. Melt butter in 8-inch FRY PAN; sauté bread cubes until brown, stirring with TURNING FORK; blend into corn pudding.
9. Pour pudding into greased 2-quart casserole; bake 1 hour at 350° F.
10. Eight servings.

90

Cottage Potatoes

2 medium potatoes
3 large sprigs parsley
Salt, pepper
1 tablespoon butter or margarine
¼ cup light cream
Grated Parmesan cheese

1. Pare potatoes using PARING KNIFE; cut into ⅜-inch strips using FRENCH CHEF'S KNIFE.
2. Snip parsley using KITCHEN SHEARS.
3. Place potato strips in center of double thick square of Alcoa Wrap; sprinkle with parsley, salt, pepper; dot with butter; pour on cream; sprinkle top with Parmesan cheese.
4. Bring torn edges of foil together; fold in tight double folds over top and at each end.
5. Place foil package on baking sheet; bake 40–45 minutes at 425° F.
6. Two–three servings.

Cottage Cheese Herbed Onions

2 pounds whole small onions
¼ cup butter or margarine
¼ cup flour
½ cup milk
½ teaspoon salt
Dash pepper
1 teaspoon marjoram
1½ cups cottage cheese, cream style
1½ cups buttered fresh bread crumbs

1. Peel onions using PARING KNIFE; cook in boiling salted water 20 minutes or until tender; drain.
2. Place onions in greased 2-quart casserole.
3. Melt butter in 1-quart SAUCE PAN; blend in flour using MIX-STIR; add milk; cook until thick, stirring constantly.
4. Quickly blend in salt, pepper, marjoram, cottage cheese; spread over onions using SPREADER SPATULA; top with buttered crumbs.
5. Bake 25 minutes at 375° F.
6. Six servings.

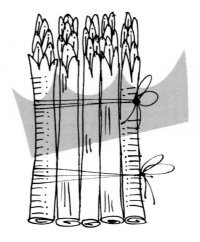

Asparagus à la King

1 pound fresh asparagus
4 hard cooked eggs
¼ cup butter or margarine
¼ cup flour
2 cups milk
½ teaspoon salt
Dash pepper
1 teaspoon leaf oregano
2 cups grated Cheddar cheese

1. Wash asparagus; cut into 1-inch pieces using FRENCH CHEF'S KNIFE.
2. Cook asparagus until just tender; set aside.
3. Dice eggs using FRENCH CHEF'S KNIFE.
4. Melt butter in 3-quart SAUCE PAN; add flour, blending with MIX-STIR.
5. Add milk; cook over low heat stirring constantly until thickened.
6. Add salt, pepper, oregano, cheese; stir until cheese melts.
7. Add asparagus, eggs; blend well; heat 5 minutes.
8. Serve in patty shells or over chow mein noodles.
9. Five–six servings.

Vegetables

Chow String Beans with Sour Cream

2 10-ounce packages frozen cut green beans
¼ cup vegetable oil
3 tablespoons chopped onion
1 teaspoon flour
1 tablespoon water
½ teaspoon salt
⅛ teaspoon pepper
¼ teaspoon grated lemon peel
1½ tablespoons chopped parsley
½ cup dairy sour cream
2 tablespoons cornflake crumbs
¼ cup grated Cheddar cheese

1. Thaw green beans.
2. Heat oil in 10-inch FRY PAN over medium-high heat; add green beans, onions; cook stirring constantly 1 minute using TURNING FORK; cover; cook additional 1 minute. (Note: Beans should be bright green with crisp, crunchy texture.)
3. Stir in flour; add water, salt, pepper, lemon peel, parsley, sour cream; blend thoroughly.
4. Pour into 1-quart casserole; sprinkle with cornflake crumbs; top with grated cheese.
5. Bake 20 minutes at 350° F.
6. Six servings.

Sweet Potato Balls

2 cups mashed sweet potatoes
2 tablespoons flour
2 tablespoons sugar
1 egg, beaten
1 quart oil for frying
Confectioners' Sugar

1. Combine potatoes, flour, sugar, egg; blend together using TURNING FORK.
2. Form mixture in balls, 1-inch in diameter.
3. Pour oil into 10-inch FRY PAN; heat to 375° F.
4. Drop potato balls into hot oil; fry to golden brown, turning with TURNING FORK; remove using PERFORATED SPOON; drain on paper toweling.
5. Sprinkle with confectioners' sugar; serve hot.
6. Four servings.

Italian Rice with Peas

1 small onion
3 tablespoons butter or margarine
¾ cup raw rice
½ 10-ounce package frozen peas
1 cup diced cooked ham
2½ cups canned chicken broth
1 tablespoon butter or margarine
¼ cup grated Parmesan cheese

1. Peel onion using PARING KNIFE; chop using FRENCH CHEF'S KNIFE.
2. Melt butter in 2-quart SAUCE PAN; sauté onions over medium heat 2-3 minutes, stirring with TURNING FORK.
3. Stir in rice, peas, ham, chicken broth; bring to boil.
4. Cover; simmer 15–20 minutes or until all broth is absorbed.
5. Stir in butter, cheese.
6. Six servings.

Dublin Cheese and Potato Pie

    4 medium potatoes
    2 medium onions
    1 cup milk
    1 cup grated Cheddar cheese
    1 teaspoon Worcestershire sauce
    1 teaspoon salt
    ¼ teaspoon pepper
    1 tablespoon flour
    3 tablespoons butter or margarine
    2 tablespoons dry bread crumbs

1. Pare potatoes using PARING KNIFE; cut into ⅛-inch slices using FRENCH CHEF'S KNIFE.
2. Peel onions using PARING KNIFE; cut into thin slices using TRIMMER.
3. Combine milk, cheese in 1-quart SAUCE PAN; heat over low heat until cheese melts; stir constantly with MIX-STIR; add Worcestershire sauce.
4. Combine salt, pepper, flour.
5. Place layer of sliced potatoes in bottom of greased 1½-quart casserole; sprinkle one half of flour mixture over top; add layer of onions; dot with half of butter; repeat layers using remaining ingredients.
6. Pour cheese sauce over all; top with bread crumbs.
7. Bake 1 hour at 350° F.
8. Four–five servings.

Rarebit Stuffed Peppers

    3 large green peppers
    ½ pound Cheddar cheese
    2 tablespoons butter or margarine
    2 tablespoons minced onion
    1 No. 2 can kidney beans, drained
    2 tablespoons ketchup
    ½ teaspoon Worcestershire sauce
    ½ teaspoon salt
      Dash pepper

1. Cut green peppers in half lengthwise using TRIMMER; remove seeds; panbroil 5 minutes; drain.
2. Cut cheese into small cubes using FRENCH CHEF'S KNIFE.
3. Melt butter in 10-inch FRY PAN; sauté onion until tender, stirring with TURNING FORK; remove from heat.
4. Add cheese, kidney beans, ketchup, Worcestershire sauce, salt, pepper; blend.
5. Fill peppers with cheese mixture; place filled peppers in 9 x 13-inch bake pan.
6. Bake 30 minutes at 350° F.
7. Six servings.

Sauces

Foo Yung Sauce (China)

1 cup canned chicken broth
⅓ cup frozen peas, thawed
1 tablespoon cornstarch
2 tablespoons canned chicken broth
1 tablespoon soy sauce

1. Combine chicken broth, peas in 1-quart SAUCE PAN; bring to boil; simmer 3 minutes.
2. Dissolve cornstarch in 2 tablespoons chicken broth; blend into hot broth using MIX-STIR.
3. Add soy sauce; cook 2 minutes, stirring constantly.
4. Serve over Egg Foo Yung.
5. About 1 cup sauce.

Lemon Cucumber Sauce

2 egg yolks
¼ cup lemon juice
½ cup butter or margarine
½ cup well-drained, grated cucumber

1. Beat egg yolks slightly in 1-quart SAUCE PAN using MIX-STIR.
2. Add lemon juice, ¼ cup butter; stir over low heat until blended.
3. Add remaining ¼ cup butter; continue cooking, stirring constantly, until thickened, smooth.
4. Stir in grated cucumber.
5. Serve over Salmon Casserole.
6. About 1 cup sauce.

Chateau Sauce (France)

1 small onion
2 tablespoons pickled onions
¼ cup butter or margarine
¼ cup flour
6 beef bouillon cubes
3 cups boiling water
⅓ cup tomato purée
2 tablespoons bottled meat sauce
¼ cup chopped canned mushrooms
¼ cup white wine
½ cup butter or margarine

1. Peel onion using PARING KNIFE; chop onion, pickled onions using FRENCH CHEF'S KNIFE.
2. Melt butter in 10-inch FRY PAN; sauté onions until lightly browned, stirring with TURNING FORK.
3. Blend in flour using MIX-STIR; cook over medium heat 8–9 minutes or until browned, stirring constantly.
4. Dissolve bouillon cubes in boiling water; stir in tomato purée, meat sauce; add to sautéed onions; blend well.
5. Cook over medium heat about 10 minutes or until thickened, stirring constantly.
6. Combine mushrooms, wine in 1-quart SAUCE PAN; cook uncovered over medium heat until liquid has evaporated; add to sauce.
7. Add butter; blend thoroughly.
8. Serve with meat.
9. About 4 cups sauce.

Sauces

Sweet-Sour Sauce (Polynesia)

1 tablespoon butter or margarine
1 cup water
½ cup cider vinegar
3 tablespoons soy sauce
¼ cup sugar
1 tablespoon cornstarch
3 tablespoons sherry wine

1. Melt butter in 2-quart SAUCE PAN; add water, vinegar, soy sauce, sugar; blend thoroughly using MIX-STIR; bring to boil; simmer 5 minutes.
2. Dissolve cornstarch in sherry; slowly stir into simmering liquid.
3. Simmer, stirring constantly until thickened.
4. Serve with pork, spareribs.
5. About 2 cups sauce.

Parsley Sauce (Denmark)

2 tablespoons butter or margarine
2 tablespoons flour
1 cup canned chicken broth
¼ teaspoon salt
1 teaspoon lemon juice
1 teaspoon grated lemon peel
2 tablespoons chopped parsley

1. Melt butter in 1-quart SAUCE PAN; stir in flour using MIX-STIR; cook over low heat 2 minutes.
2. Gradually stir in broth, salt; cook over low heat until thickened, stirring constantly.
3. Add lemon juice, lemon peel, parsley; blend well.
4. Serve with fish.
5. About 1 cup sauce.

Mexican Chili Sauce

2 8-ounce cans tomato purée
¼ cup tomato paste
¾ cup canned chicken broth
¼ cup instant chopped onion
1 teaspoon chili powder
½ teaspoon cinnamon
½ teaspoon ground cloves
½ teaspoon ground coriander
⅛ teaspoon instant minced garlic
1 tablespoon sugar
1 teaspoon salt
¼ teaspoon pepper
1 1-ounce square unsweetened chocolate

1. Combine all ingredients except chocolate in 2-quart SAUCE PAN; blend thoroughly using MIX-STIR.
2. Bring to boil over medium heat; add chocolate; simmer over low heat until chocolate melts; stir frequently.
3. Serve with roast turkey, chicken or pork.
4. About 4 cups sauce.

Sauce Béarnaise (France)

1 teaspoon tarragon
1 teaspoon chervil
2 tablespoons finely chopped
    scallions
4 whole black peppercorns, ground
¼ cup tarragon vinegar
¼ cup white wine
3 egg yolks
1 tablespoon water
½ pound butter or margarine
1 teaspoon salt
¼ teaspoon cayenne

1. Combine tarragon, chervil, scallions, ground pepper, vinegar, wine in 1-quart SAUCE PAN; blend well using MIX-STIR.
2. Cook over medium heat until reduced to a thick paste, stirring constantly; remove from heat; cool slightly.
3. Combine egg yolks, water; blend well using MIX-STIR; add to seasoned paste, beating until light, fluffy.
4. Place over low heat; add butter in thirds, beating well after each addition.
5. Add salt, cayenne; blend well.
6. Serve with broiled fish.
7. About 1 cup sauce.

Raisin Sauce

½ cup brown sugar, firmly packed
1½ teaspoons dry mustard
1½ tablespoons flour
½ cup seedless raisins
¼ cup vinegar
1¾ cups water

1. Combine all ingredients in 1-quart SAUCE PAN; blend thoroughly using MIX-STIR.
2. Bring to boil over medium heat; simmer 15 minutes over low heat; stir occasionally.
3. Serve with ham or fresh pork.
4. About 2 cups sauce.

Steak Sauce

6 tablespoons butter or margarine
6 tablespoons lemon juice
1 teaspoon dry mustard
2 tablespoons Worcestershire sauce
Salt, pepper

1. Melt butter in 1-quart SAUCE PAN; blend in remaining ingredients using MIX-STIR; simmer 5 minutes.
2. Serve with broiled steaks.
3. About ½ cup sauce.

Mint Sauce

Fresh mint
½ cup vinegar
1 cup water
¼ cup lemon juice
½ cup water
2 tablespoons sugar
¼ teaspoon salt

1. Snip enough fresh mint to make ½ cup using KITCHEN SHEARS.
2. Add ¼ cup mint to 1-quart SAUCE PAN along with vinegar, 1 cup water; simmer until liquid is reduced one half; strain.
3. Add lemon juice, the ½ cup water, sugar, salt; blend using MIX-STIR; chill.
4. Just before serving add remaining ¼ cup mint.
5. Serve with cold roast lamb.
6. About 1 cup sauce.

Sauces

Allemande Sauce (France)

3 tablespoons butter or margarine
2 tablespoons flour
1 cup canned chicken broth
¼ teaspoon salt
¼ teaspoon paprika
1 egg yolk
1 teaspoon lemon juice

1. Melt butter in 1-quart SAUCE PAN over medium heat; stir in flour using MIX-STIR; gradually add broth; blend well.
2. Cook over low heat until thickened, stirring constantly.
3. Add salt, paprika, egg yolk; beat thoroughly; continue cooking 1–2 minutes, stirring constantly.
4. Stir in lemon juice.
5. Serve with asparagus or green beans.
6. About 1 cup sauce.

Egg-Lemon Sauce (Greece)

4 eggs
2 tablespoons lemon juice
1 cup hot canned chicken broth
½ teaspoon salt
Dash white pepper

1. Beat eggs in 1-quart SAUCE PAN using MIX-STIR; gradually blend in lemon juice.
2. Slowly add hot chicken broth, beating constantly; add salt, pepper.
3. Cook over low heat 5–8 minutes or until thickened; stir constantly; do not boil.
4. Serve with broccoli, asparagus, green beans, artichoke hearts.
5. About 1½ cups sauce.

White Clam Sauce (Italy)

3 cloves garlic
2 large sprigs parsley
2 tablespoons olive oil
1 cup canned clam juice
¼ teaspoon salt
Dash pepper
2 7½-ounce cans minced clams, drained

1. Mince garlic cloves using FRENCH CHEF'S KNIFE.
2. Snip parsley using KITCHEN SHEARS.
3. Heat oil in 1-quart SAUCE PAN; sauté garlic 3 minutes over medium heat, stirring with TURNING FORK.
4. Add parsley, clam juice, salt, pepper; simmer 10 minutes.
5. Add clams; simmer 2 minutes.
6. Serve with spaghetti.
7. About 2 cups sauce.

Variation: For Red Clam Sauce, add ¼ cup tomato paste.

Old-Fashioned Lemon Sauce

½ cup butter or margarine
1 cup sugar
¼ cup water
1 egg
3 tablespoons lemon juice
Grated peel of 1 lemon

1. Combine all ingredients in 1-quart SAUCE PAN; blend thoroughly using MIX-STIR.
2. Cook over medium heat, stirring constantly, just until mixture comes to a boil.
3. Serve warm over Blueberry Buckle, gingerbread.
4. About 1⅓ cups sauce.

Ginger Sauce (Lebanon)

½ cup sugar
2 tablespoons cornstarch
⅛ teaspoon nutmeg
½ teaspoon ginger
  Grated peel of 1 lemon
1¼ cups pineapple juice
1 12-ounce can apricot nectar
2 tablespoons lemon juice

1. Combine sugar, cornstarch, nutmeg, ginger, lemon peel in 2-quart SAUCE PAN; blend together with MIX-STIR.
2. Add pineapple juice, apricot nectar, lemon juice; stir until smooth.
3. Bring to a boil; cook over low heat, stirring constantly, about 10 minutes or until smooth, thickened.
4. Cool, stirring occasionally to prevent film from forming.
5. Store in covered container in refrigerator.
6. Serve cold with fresh, canned, or frozen fruits.
7. About 3 cups sauce.

Almond Apricot Sauce

2 cups dried apricots
2 cups water
½ cup sugar
1 teaspoon lemon juice
½ cup slivered blanched almonds

1. Cut apricots into eighths using KITCHEN SHEARS.
2. Place in 2-quart SAUCE PAN along with water; simmer about 20 minutes or until apricots are tender.
3. Add sugar, lemon juice, almonds; stir.
4. Serve warm over plain sponge cake or pound cake.
5. About 2½ cups sauce.

Nutmeg Sauce

¼ cup butter or margarine
1½ tablespoons flour
½ cup sugar
1 egg yolk
1 teaspoon vanilla
1¼ cups boiling water
¼ teaspoon nutmeg

1. Melt butter in 1-quart SAUCE PAN; remove from heat; blend in flour, sugar using MIX-STIR.
2. Blend in egg yolk, vanilla; gradually add boiling water, blending thoroughly.
3. Cook over low heat, stirring constantly, until thickened.
4. Stir in nutmeg.
5. Serve warm over gingerbread, spice cake.
6. About 2 cups sauce.

Rum Sauce

2 eggs
1 cup sugar
1 cup heavy cream, whipped
  Rum or rum extract

1. Beat eggs until light using MIX-STIR.
2. Add sugar gradually, continuing to beat until mixture loses its grainy texture.
3. Fold into whipped cream; flavor to taste with rum or rum extract
4. Serve over plum pudding, apple crisp.
5. About 1½ cups sauce.

Desserts

Danish Apple Cake

- 2 pounds cooking apples
- ¼ cup sugar
- ½ cup water
- 1 teaspoon vanilla
- 2 cups dry bread crumbs
- 1 cup oatmeal, uncooked
- ¼ cup brown sugar, firmly packed
- 1 teaspoon cinnamon
- 1 cup butter or margarine, melted
- ¾ cup strawberry preserves

1. Pare, quarter, core apples using PARING KNIFE; slice using TRIMMER.
2. Combine apple slices, sugar, water, vanilla in 2-quart SAUCE PAN; bring to boil; simmer 5–10 minutes or until apples are just tender; cool slightly.
3. In bowl combine bread crumbs, oatmeal, brown sugar, cinnamon.
4. Spread ½ the crumb mixture in bottom of greased 9-inch square bake pan; top with apples; pour ½ cup melted butter over apples.
5. Spread preserves over apples using SPREADER SPATULA; top with remaining crumb mixture, melted butter.
6. Bake 30 minutes at 400° F.
7. Serve warm.
8. Eight–nine servings.

Norwegian Fruit Dessert

- 2 oranges
- 1 small banana
- ¾ cup seedless white grapes
- 2 ounces shelled walnuts
- 1 small red apple
- 1 teaspoon lemon juice
- 1 teaspoon water
- 3 eggs
- 3 tablespoons sugar
- ½ tablespoon brandy or rum

1. Peel oranges using TRIMMER; separate into sections.
2. Peel banana; coarsely chop using FRENCH CHEF'S KNIFE.
3. Cut grapes in half using PARING KNIFE.
4. Chop walnuts using FRENCH CHEF'S KNIFE.
5. Cut apple in quarters using TRIMMER; core using PARING KNIFE; coarsely chop using FRENCH CHEF'S KNIFE; sprinkle with diluted lemon juice.
6. Combine fruits, walnuts; refrigerate.
7. When ready to serve, beat eggs until soft peaks form; gradually beat in sugar, brandy.
8. Serve sauce over chilled fruit mixture.
9. Six servings.

Desserts

Deep Dish Apple-Cheese Pie

Pastry for 1 crust 8-inch square pan
4 medium apples
¼ cup sugar
¼ teaspoon cinnamon
¼ teaspoon nutmeg
2 eggs
½ cup sugar
⅛ teaspoon salt
1 cup milk, scalded
1 teaspoon vanilla
1 cup creamed cottage cheese

1. Line 8-inch square bake pan with pastry; flute edges.
2. Pare, quarter, core apples using PARING KNIFE; slice thinly using TRIMMER; arrange slices in pastry shell.
3. Combine sugar, cinnamon, nutmeg; sprinkle over apples.
4. Bake 15 minutes at 425° F.; remove from oven; reduce temperature to 325° F.
5. Beat eggs using MIX-STIR; add sugar, salt, milk, vanilla, cottage cheese; blend thoroughly.
6. Pour cheese mixture over apples; spread evenly using SPREADER SPATULA.
7. Bake 40–50 minutes at 325° F.
8. Cool before serving.
9. Six servings.

Rhubarb Custard Pie

Pastry for 1 crust 9-inch pie
Pastry for lattice strips
1¼ pounds fresh rhubarb
3 eggs
3 tablespoons milk
2 cups sugar
¼ cup flour
¾ teaspoon nutmeg
1 tablespoon butter or margarine

1. Line 9-inch pie pan with pastry; flute edge.
2. Trim root, leaf ends of rhubarb using TRIMMER; cut stocks into 1-inch pieces (to make 4 cups) using FRENCH CHEF'S KNIFE; arrange in pie shell.
3. Beat eggs, milk using MIX-STIR; add sugar, flour, nutmeg; blend thoroughly.
4. Pour egg mixture over rhubarb; dot with butter; arrange lattice strips over top.
5. Bake 50–60 minutes at 400° F. or until nicely browned.
6. Serve warm.
7. Six–seven servings.

Southern Pecan Pie

Pastry for 1 crust 9-inch pie
½ cup butter or margarine
½ cup sugar
3 eggs
¾ cup white corn syrup
2 tablespoons honey
1 teaspoon vanilla
2 cups pecan halves

1. Line 9-inch pie pan with pastry; flute edge.
2. Cream butter until soft; add sugar gradually, continuing to beat until light, fluffy.
3. Beat eggs using MIX-STIR; add syrup, honey, vanilla; blend thoroughly.
4. Slowly beat egg mixture into butter-sugar mixture; add 1 cup pecans.
5. Pour into pie shell; arrange remaining 1 cup pecans on top.
6. Bake 50–55 minutes at 350° F.; cool.
7. Top with whipped cream if desired.
8. Six–seven servings.

Black Bottom Pie

Vanilla Wafer Crust:
1⅓ cups fine vanilla wafer crumbs
   (about 24)
¼ cup soft butter or margarine
¼ cup sugar

Filling:
 4 egg yolks
 1 cup milk
 1 cup light cream
 ½ cup sugar
 4 teaspoons cornstarch
1½ squares unsweetened chocolate,
   melted
 ½ teaspoon vanilla
 1 tablespoon unflavored gelatin
 ¼ cup cold water
 1 tablespoon rum
 3 egg whites
 ¼ teaspoon salt
 ¼ teaspoon cream of tartar
 ¼ cup sugar

1. Combine wafer crumbs, butter, sugar; blend together with TURNING FORK until crumbly.

2. Pour into 9-inch pie pan; press crumbs evenly, firmly to bottom, sides of pan.

3. Bake 8 minutes at 375° F.; cool.

4. Combine egg yolks, milk, cream in 1-quart SAUCE PAN; beat thoroughly using MIX-STIR.

5. Combine sugar, cornstarch; blend into milk mixture; cook over low heat about 20 minutes or until mixture coats spoon heavily; stir occasionally.

6. Remove 1 cup custard; add melted chocolate, vanilla to it; beat until cool; pour into prepared shell; spread evenly using SPREADER SPATULA.

7. Stir gelatin into water; add to remaining custard; stir until dissolved; cool slightly; stir in rum.

8. Beat egg whites, salt until frothy; add cream of tartar; beat until stiff; beat in sugar, 1 tablespoon at a time.

9. Fold gelatin-custard mixture into egg whites; pour on top of chocolate custard; spread evenly using SPREADER SPATULA; chill until firm.

10. Top with sweetened whipped cream if desired.

11. Six–seven servings.

Fresh Pear Pie (Canada)

   Pastry for 2 crust 9-inch pie
5-6 fresh pears
 ½ cup sugar
 2 tablespoons quick cooking tapioca
 ⅛ teaspoon salt
 ¼ teaspoon cinnamon
 ¼ teaspoon nutmeg
 ¼ teaspoon ginger
 1 tablespoon lemon juice

1. Line 9-inch pie pan with pastry.

2. Pare, quarter, core pears using TRIMMER; arrange slices in pie shell.

3. In small bowl combine sugar, tapioca, salt, cinnamon, nutmeg; ginger; pour over slices; sprinkle with lemon juice.

4. Cover with top crust; seal edges; flute; bake 40 minutes at 425° F.

5. Six–seven servings.

Desserts

Paradise Pie

Meringue Shell:
- 6 egg whites, room temperature
- 2 cups sugar
- 2 teaspoons vinegar
- 1½ teaspoons vanilla
- ⅛ teaspoon salt

Filling:
- 2 squares unsweetened chocolate
- ½ cup sugar
- ¼ cup cold water
- 4 egg yolks
- 1 cup butter or margarine
- 1 cup confectioners' sugar
- 4 egg whites
- 1 cup whipping cream
- 1 teaspoon vanilla

1. Beat egg whites, using electric mixer at high speed, until stiff but not dry.
2. Add one half the sugar, 2 tablespoons at a time, beating well after each addition.
3. Add vinegar, vanilla, salt; blend; add remaining sugar, beating thoroughly.
4. Pour mixture into 12-inch pizza pan; spread over bottom using SPATULA SPREADER; shape so there is a 1-inch high rim around edge.
5. Bake 1 hour at 250° F.; cool.
6. Combine chocolate, sugar, water in 3-quart SAUCE PAN; heat until melted.
7. Beat egg yolks until lemon-colored using MIX-STIR; add to chocolate mixture; cook until thick, stirring constantly; cool.
8. Cream butter, sugar together until light, fluffy; add to chocolate mixture; blend well using MIX-STIR.
9. Beat egg whites until stiff; fold into chocolate mixture; refrigerate until serving time.
10. To Serve: Fill meringue shell with chocolate mixture; whip cream; add vanilla; spread over top of chocolate filling using SPREADER SPATULA.
11. Twelve servings.

Cheese Cake

- 2 eggs
- ½ cup sugar
- 12 ounces cream cheese, softened
- ½ teaspoon vanilla
- 1 teaspoon lemon juice
- 1½ cups graham cracker crumbs
- 2 tablespoons sugar
- ¼ cup butter or margarine
- 1 cup dairy sour cream
- 2 tablespoons sugar
- ½ teaspoon vanilla
- Nutmeg

1. Beat eggs until light using MIX-STIR; add sugar gradually, beating after each addition.
2. Add cream cheese, vanilla, lemon juice; beat thoroughly.
3. Combine cracker crumbs, sugar, butter using TURNING FORK; press onto bottom, up sides of 9-inch pie pan.
4. Pour in cheese mixture; spread evenly with SPREADER SPATULA.
5. Bake 20 minutes at 375° F.; cool 1 hour.
6. Combine sour cream, sugar, vanilla; spread evenly over cooled cake using SPREADER SPATULA.
7. Bake 10 minutes at 400° F.; sprinkle top with nutmeg; cool; chill.
8. Six–seven servings.

Pêches Cardinal (France)

6 fresh peaches
5 cups water
1½ cups sugar
2½ tablespoons vanilla
1 10-ounce package frozen red
   raspberries, thawed, drained
1½ tablespoons confectioners' sugar
1 tablespoon brandy or kirsch
   Sweetened whipped cream

1. Pare peaches using PARING KNIFE; cut in half using TRIMMER; remove pits.
2. Combine water, sugar in 3-quart SAUCE PAN; bring to a boil; boil 4 minutes, stirring until sugar dissolves.
3. Add vanilla, peach halves; simmer slowly for 10–15 minutes until peaches are just tender.
4. Cool; cover; refrigerate until cold.
5. Purée raspberries in electric blender; put liquid through sieve to remove seeds.
6. Add sugar, brandy to purée; blend well; cover; refrigerate.
7. To serve: Remove peach halves from syrup using PERFORATED SPOON; place in individual dessert dishes; cover with raspberry sauce; garnish with whipped cream.
8. Twelve servings.

Cardamom Loaf (Iceland)

1 cup butter or margarine
1 cup sugar
2 eggs
3 cups sifted all purpose flour
3 teaspoons baking powder
½ teaspoon salt
1 teaspoon ground cardamom
¾ cup milk
1 cup seedless raisins

1. Cream butter; add sugar gradually, continuing to cream until light, fluffy.
2. Add eggs; beat well.
3. Sift together flour, baking powder, salt, cardamom; add to butter mixture; mix well.
4. Blend in milk; fold in raisins.
5. Pour into greased, floured 9 x 5 x 3-inch loaf pan.
6. Bake 70 minutes at 375° F.
7. Slice thin to serve using SLICER.
8. Serve with fresh fruit if desired.
9. One medium loaf.

Belgian Apple Fritters

1 egg
1 cup flour
1 tablespoon sugar
¾ cup flat beer
½ tablespoon brandy
6 firm cooking apples
   Vegetable oil
½ cup sugar
1 teaspoon cinnamon

1. Beat egg using MIX-STIR; blend in ¼ cup flour, sugar.
2. Add beer alternately with remaining flour, beating well after each addition; blend in brandy.
3. Let batter stand at room temperature at least one hour.
4. To prepare Fritters: Pare apples using PARING KNIFE; core; cut in ¼-inch rings using TRIMMER.
5. Pour 1 inch of oil into 10-inch FRY PAN; heat oil to 375° F.
6. Coat apple rings with batter; fry in hot oil until lightly browned on both sides; remove with PERFORATED SPOON; drain on paper toweling.
7. Combine sugar, cinnamon; sprinkle over fritters.
8. Keep warm, crisp in 250° F. oven until all fritters are cooked; serve immediately.
9. Eight–ten servings.

Desserts

Canadian Apple Kuchen

2 cups sifted all purpose flour
½ teaspoon salt
¼ teaspoon baking powder
2 tablespoons sugar
6 tablespoons butter or margarine
4–5 apples
⅓ cup golden raisins
¾ cup sugar
1 teaspoon cinnamon
¼ teaspoon nutmeg
2 egg yolks
1 cup dairy sour cream

1. Sift together flour, salt, baking powder, sugar.
2. Cut in butter with 2 knives or pastry blender until mixture looks like corn meal.
3. Pile into ungreased 8-inch square cake pan; pat an even layer over bottom, halfway up sides of pan.
4. Pare apples, core using PARING KNIFE; cut in thin slices using TRIMMER; arrange in pastry shell.
5. Sprinkle raisins over apples.
6. Combine sugar, cinnamon, nutmeg; sprinkle over top.
7. Bake 15 minutes at 400° F.
8. Beat egg yolks slightly using MIX-STIR; blend in sour cream; pour over kuchen, spreading evenly with SPREADER SPATULA.
9. Bake 30 minutes longer.
10. Serve warm.
11. Six–eight servings.

Variation: For Peach Kuchen, use 12 peach halves and eliminate raisins.

Banana Flambé (Brazil)

4 ripe bananas
3 tablespoons butter or margarine
1 tablespoon grated orange peel
1 tablespoon brown sugar
1 10-ounce package frozen red
    raspberries, thawed
2 tablespoons brandy
  Brandy

1. Peel bananas; cut in half lengthwise using TRIMMER.
2. Melt butter in 10-inch FRY PAN; stir in orange peel, brown sugar using MIX-STIR; bring to boil.
3. Sauté banana halves on both sides about 3 minutes total, turning with TURNING FORK.
4. Purée raspberries in electric blender; add brandy; pour over bananas; heat.
5. To serve: Pour 2 tablespoons warmed brandy into LADLE; ignite; pour over bananas; when flame dies out, serve.
6. Four servings.

Blueberry Buckle

¾ cup sugar
¼ cup shortening
1 egg
½ cup milk
2 cups sifted all purpose flour
2 teaspoons baking powder
½ teaspoon salt
1 cup blueberries, well-drained
½ cup sugar
⅓ cup sifted all purpose flour
½ teaspoon cinnamon
¼ cup soft butter or margarine

1. Beat together sugar, shortening, egg; stir in milk.
2. Sift together flour, baking powder, salt; stir into sugar mixture.
3. Carefully blend in blueberries.
4. Pour batter into greased, floured 9-inch square bake pan; spread evenly using SPREADER SPATULA.
5. Combine sugar, flour, cinnamon, butter using TURNING FORK; sprinkle over batter.
6. Bake 45–50 minutes at 375° F.
7. Serve warm with Old-Fashioned Lemon Sauce.
8. Nine servings.

Swiss Fir Cone
(Cake for Christmas Season)

Sponge Cake:
¾ cup sugar
4 eggs
Grated peel of one lemon
¼ cup sifted all purpose flour
¼ cup cornstarch
½ teaspoon baking powder

1. Combine sugar, eggs in large mixing bowl; set in deep pan or bowl of warm water.
2. Beat 15 minutes with electric mixer; remove from warm water; beat another 5 minutes; add grated lemon peel.
3. Sift flour, cornstarch, baking powder together; fold into egg mixture.
4. Line bottom, sides of 15 x 10 x 1-inch bake pan with waxed paper; pour in batter; spread evenly using SPREADER SPATULA.
5. Bake 30–35 minutes at 350° F.
6. When cake is removed from oven, loosen around edges with SPREADER SPATULA; turn upside down on cooling racks; remove pan; quickly peel off paper.

Coffee Butter Cream Frosting:
1¼ cups butter or margarine
2 cups sifted confectioners' sugar
½ cup strong coffee
2 cups blanched almonds, split, toasted

1. Cream butter until fluffy; add sugar gradually, blending well.
2. Add coffee; beat until creamy.

Assembling Fir Cone:
1. Cut three patterns from double thickness of Alcoa Wrap using bottom of an ordinary iron to obtain shape. Dimensions should be:
   #1, 9½ inches in length, 6 inches at broad end.
   #2, 9 inches by 5½ inches.
   #3, 8 inches by 4 inches.

2. Arrange patterns on cake; cut around patterns using TRIMMER to make fir cone shapes.
3. Assemble fir cone using largest cone shape for base; frost between each layer, around sides and over top with Coffee Butter Cream Frosting using SPREADER SPATULA.
4. Beginning at point of cake, place toasted split almonds into frosting in overlapping pattern to resemble fir cone scales.
5. Sprinkle confectioners' sugar lightly over entire surface to resemble snow.
6. At blunt end, fasten small twig of fir branch, red ribbon bow.
7. Eight–ten servings.

Rum Balls

2 tablespoons cocoa
1 cup confectioners' sugar
¼ cup light rum
2 tablespoons light corn syrup
2½ cups vanilla wafer crumbs
1 cup chopped pecans

1. Sift cocoa, confectioners' sugar together; blend in rum, corn syrup.
2. Add wafer crumbs, pecans; mix thoroughly using TURNING FORK.
3. Form mixture into 1-inch balls; roll in confectioners' sugar.
4. About 2½–3 dozen balls.

Variation: For Bourbon Balls, substitute bourbon for rum.

Desserts

Cottage Cheese Cookie Sticks

1 cup creamed cottage cheese
1 cup butter or margarine
2 cups sifted all purpose flour
¼ cup melted butter or margarine
¾ cup finely chopped walnuts
¾ cup brown sugar, firmly packed

1. Blend cottage cheese, butter together with pastry cutter.
2. Blend flour into mixture until dough holds together.
3. Roll out on lightly floured board to ⅛-inch thickness.
4. Brush melted butter over dough; sprinkle walnuts, brown sugar over entire surface.
5. Cut into equal strips, about 3 inches wide using SPATULA SPREADER; cut each strip into triangles, each about 3 inches wide at base.
6. Lift triangles from board using SPATULA SPREADER; beginning at base of triangle, roll dough into sticks.
7. Place sticks on ungreased cookie sheet, point side down.
8. Bake 20 minutes at 400° F. or until golden brown.
9. About 4–4½ dozen cookies.

Nut Pie

4 egg whites
½ cup granulated sugar
½ cup light brown sugar,
    firmly packed
½ teaspoon salt
1 teaspoon vanilla
¾ cup crushed round crackers
    (about 21)
¾ cup chopped nuts
1 teaspoon baking powder

1. Beat egg whites until stiff but not dry.
2. Gradually add sugars, continuing to beat until thoroughly blended, stiff.
3. Add salt, vanilla; blend.

4. Combine cracker crumbs, nuts, baking powder; fold into egg white mixture.
5. Pour into ungreased 9-inch pie pan; spread evenly using SPREADER SPATULA.
6. Bake 30 minutes at 325° F.
7. To serve: Fill with ice cream; top with whipped cream.
8. Six servings.

Pineapple Fritters

¼ cup flour
2 eggs
½ teaspoon salt
6 pineapple slices
Vegetable shortening
Confectioners' sugar

1. Blend flour, eggs, salt together to make batter using MIX-STIR.
2. Cut pineapple slices in half using TRIMMER; drain on paper toweling.
3. Pour 1 inch of oil in 10-inch FRY PAN; heat oil to 375° F.
4. Coat pineapple slices with batter; fry in hot oil until lightly browned on both sides; remove with PERFORATED SPOON; drain on paper toweling.
5. Sprinkle with confectioners' sugar; serve hot.
6. Six servings.

Fruit Medley

ups crisp macaroon crumbs
(about 40)
o. 303 can sliced peaches, drained
-pound can pitted purple plums,
drained
o. 2 can pineapple chunks,
drained
-pound can pitted Bing Cherries,
drained
up sherry wine

ightly grease 9-inch square bake
an; sprinkle ½ cup macaroon
rumbs in bottom.
Combine peaches, plums, pineap-
le, cherries; toss together using
TURNING FORK.
Spoon layer of fruit into pan using
SOLID SPOON; sprinkle with
rumbs.
Continue layering fruit, crumbs,
ending with layer of crumbs.
Pour sherry over top of crumbs.
Bake 40–45 minutes at 350° F.
Serve warm topped with sweet-
ened whipped cream or dairy sour
cream, if desired.
Six–eight servings.

tch Shortbread

cup butter or margarine
cup + 2 tablespoons sugar
egg yolk
cups sifted all purpose flour

Cream butter until soft; add sugar
gradually; beat until light, fluffy;
blend in egg yolk.
Add flour in three additions, beating well after each addition.
Divide mixture in half; roll out
each half on lightly floured board
to ½-inch thickness (about 7
inches in diameter); place in bottom of two 9-inch pie pans.
Score each round into 8 pie-shaped
wedges using TRIMMER; pierce
with TURNING FORK in several
places over top.
Bake 25 minutes at 325° F.; separate into wedges using TRIM-
MER; cool on rack.
Sixteen servings.

Fruit Curry

⅓ cup butter or margarine
¾ cup light brown sugar, firmly
packed
1 tablespoon curry powder
1 No. 2 can peach halves, drained
1 No. 2 can pear halves, drained
1 No. 2 can pineapple chunks, drained
12 maraschino cherries, drained

1. Melt butter in 1-quart SAUCE
PAN; add brown sugar, curry;
blend well using MIX-STIR.
2. Arrange peaches, pears, pineapple
in 9-inch square bake pan; place
cherries in peach and pear centers; spoon syrup over fruit using
SOLID SPOON.
3. Bake 45 minutes at 350° F.
4. Serve warm.
5. Six–eight servings.

Raspberry Cream Parfait

3 tablespoons quick cooking tapioca
¼ cup sugar
¼ teaspoon salt
1⅓ cups milk
½ cup heavy cream
2 cups fresh red raspberries
2 tablespoons sugar

1. Mix tapioca, sugar, salt in 1-quart
SAUCE PAN using MIX-STIR.
2. Add milk gradually; cook, stirring constantly until mixture
boils.
3. Remove from heat; cool.
4. Whip cream; fold into tapioca
mixture; chill.
5. Crush raspberries slightly using
MIX-STIR; add sugar.
6. Spoon raspberries, tapioca mixture into parfait glasses in alternate layers.
7. Serve plain or topped with
whipped cream.
8. Four servings.

Variation: Fresh strawberries, black
raspberries, etc., may be substituted
for red raspberries.

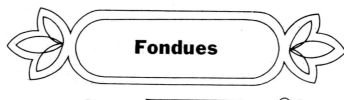

Fondues

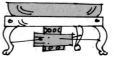

Fondue Bourguigonne (Beef Fondue)

2 pounds beef tenderloin, ¾-inch thick
2 cups vegetable oil
Variety of sauces and side dishes

1. Cut beef in ¾-inch cubes using PETITE CARVER; arrange on platter lined with lettuce; garnish with parsley.
2. Pour oil into FONDUE PAN; heat on range to 400° F.
3. Place FONDUE PAN on stand; place adapter in pan; light alcohol burner; adjust burner to have 3 small holes closed.
4. Eight–ten servings for appetizers. Four–five servings as entrée.

To Serve:

Provide each guest with a salad plate, FONDUE FORK and regular fork. Place platter of beef cubes, salt shaker, pepper mill, sauces and accompaniments on the table near the FONDUE PAN.

To Cook and Eat:

Each guest helps himself to sauces and other accompaniments which he puts on his salad plate. He then spears a cube of beef with the FONDUE FORK and dips it into the hot oil, cooking it to his liking. (Only four fondue forks should be in the FONDUE PAN at one time.) Since the FONDUE FORK will become very hot, the guest transfers his meat to the regular fork and dips it into the sauce of his choice.

Flame beneath the pan should be kept regulated so that the oil remains hot.

Suggested Accompaniments:
Hot and mild mustards
Mixed pickles
Chutney
Pickled onions
Olives

Variations:

1. Chicken Fondue: Substitute 3 whole chicken breasts (boned and skinned) cut into ½-inch cubes.
2. Shrimp Fondue: Substitute 2 pounds medium shrimp (shelled and deveined).

Use your favorite sauce recipes or try several of the following. Combine all ingredients using MIX-STIR; chill.

Tangy Blue Cheese Sauce 1¼ cups

1 cup mayonnaise
¼ cup crumbled blue cheese
1 teaspoon lemon juice
2 tablespoons chopped parsley

Tartar Sauce 1 cup

½ cup mayonnaise
½ cup dairy sour cream
2 tablespoons sweet relish
1 tablespoon chopped chives
1 teaspoon lemon juice

Fondues

Combine all ingredients using MIX-STIR; chill.

Horseradish Sauce 1¼ cups

1 cup dairy sour cream
¼ cup chopped pimiento
2 tablespoons horseradish
2 tablespoons lemon juice
1 teaspoon sugar
4 drops Tabasco sauce

Curry Sauce 1 cup

1 cup dairy sour cream
½ cup mayonnaise
1 tablespoon chopped parsley
2 teaspoons curry powder
1 teaspoon lemon juice
½ teaspoon Worcestershire sauce
¼ teaspoon salt

Fondue Orientale

2 pounds lean, boneless pork, veal,
   or beef, ¾-inch thick
6 chicken or beef bouillon cubes
3 cups water
   Variety of sauces and side dishes

1. Cut meat in wafer-thin strips, ¾ inch x 2 inch using PETITE CARVER; roll strips; arrange on platter lined with lettuce; garnish with parsley.
2. Place bouillon cubes, water in FONDUE PAN; heat on range until cubes dissolve, bouillon boils.
3. Place FONDUE PAN on stand; place adapter in pan; light alcohol burner; adjust burner to have 3 small holes closed.
4. Eight–ten servings for appetizers. Four–five servings as entrée.

Follow the Fondue Bourguigonne cooking and eating procedures, and serve with the same sauces and accompaniments.

Flame beneath the pan should be kept regulated so that the bouillon continues to boil.

Fondue Neuchâtel (Swiss Fondue)

½ pound natural Swiss cheese, grated
2 tablespoons flour
1 clove fresh garlic
1 cup Neuchâtel wine or other light, dry wine
½ tablespoon lemon juice
2 tablespoons kirsch or brandy
   Nutmeg, pepper to taste
1 small loaf French or Italian bread, cut in cubes, with some crust on each cube

1. Coat cheese with flour.
2. Rub cut garlic clove over inside of FONDUE PAN.
3. Pour wine into pan; place on range over low heat; when air bubbles rise to surface, add lemon juice.
4. Add cheese by handfuls, stirring constantly using MIX-STIR until cheese melts.
5. Add kirsch, nutmeg, pepper; blend thoroughly.
6. Place FONDUE PAN on stand; light alcohol burner; adjust burner to have all 6 small holes closed.
7. Six–eight servings for appetizers. Three–four servings as entrée.

To Serve:

Provide each guest with a salad plate, FONDUE FORK and regular fork. Place platter of bread cubes on table near FONDUE PAN.

To Eat:

In eating the Swiss Fondue each guest spears a cube of bread on the FONDUE FORK, going through the soft side into the crust. He then dunks the bread in the fondue in a stirring motion until coated, then transfers the bread to a regular fork. Each person takes his leisurely turn in rotation. The stirring will help maintain the proper consistency of the fondue and will assure that each piece of bread is thoroughly coated with melted cheese.

Flame beneath the pan should be kept regulated so that the fondue bubbles lightly. If fondue becomes too thick, stir in a little preheated wine.

Fontina

2 tablespoons butter or margarine
3 tablespoons flour
1 cup milk
½ pound natural Swiss cheese, grated
Dash salt, nutmeg

1. Melt butter in FONDUE PAN on range; add flour; stirring until blended using MIX-STIR.
2. Gradually add milk, stirring constantly; cook several minutes over low heat.
3. Add cheese by handfuls, stirring constantly until cheese melts; add salt, nutmeg.
4. Place FONDUE PAN on stand; light alcohol burner; adjust burner to have all 6 small holes closed.
5. Six–eight servings for appetizers. Three–four servings as entrée.

The Fontina, a milder version of the typical Swiss Fondue Neuchâtel, can be enjoyed by young and old alike. Follow the same serving and eating procedures. If the Fontina becomes too thick, stir in a little pre-heated milk.

Pizza Fondue

1 envelope onion soup mix
1 15-ounce can tomato sauce
1 tablespoon Worcestershire sauce
1 teaspoon oregano
1½ cups (6 ounces) grated Cheddar cheese

1. Combine onion soup mix, tomato sauce, Worcestershire sauce, oregano in FONDUE PAN using MIX-STIR.
2. Heat on range over medium heat 5–10 minutes.
3. Add cheese by handfuls, stirring constantly until cheese melts.
4. Place FONDUE PAN on stand; light alcohol burner; adjust burner to have all 6 small holes closed.
5. Six–eight servings as hors d'oeuvre.
Three–four servings as entrée.

Follow the same serving and eating procedure as for Swiss Fondue.

German Fondue

1¼ cups sifted flour
2½ teaspoons baking powder
3 tablespoons sugar
¾ teaspoon salt
1 egg
¾ cup milk
1 1-pound package frankfurters
3 cups (1½ pints) vegetable oil
Variety of sauces and side dishes

1. Sift together flour, baking powder, sugar, salt.
2. Beat egg using MIX-STIR; blend in milk.
3. Stir egg mixture into dry ingredients until well blended; pour into attractive bowl.
4. Cut each frankfurter into eight slices using TRIMMER; arrange on platter lined with lettuce; garnish with parsley.
5. Heat oil to 400° F. in FONDUE PAN on range.
6. Place FONDUE PAN on stand; place adapter in pan; light alcohol burner; adjust burner to have 3 small holes closed.
7. Eight–ten servings as hors d'oeuvre.
Four–five servings as entrée.

To Serve:
Provide each guest with salad plate, FONDUE FORK, regular fork. Place bowl of batter, platter of frankfurters, sauces and side dishes on table near FONDUE PAN. Each guest helps himself to the sauces which he puts on his salad plate; then spears a slice of frankfurter with the FONDUE FORK, coats it with batter and cooks it in the hot oil. He transfers the cooked "fritter" to a regular fork and dips it in the sauces of his choice.

Suggested Sauces and Side Dishes:
Hot and mild mustards
Mustard-Dill Sauce
Tomato Sauce
Ketchup
Pancake Syrup

Fondues

Italian Bagna Cauda

This hot garlic-anchovy dip is a popular Italian specialty. It can be served as an hors d'oeuvre or an entrée.

8 cloves garlic, minced
¼ cup butter or margarine
1 2-ounce flat can anchovy fillets, finely chopped
1 cup olive oil
Assorted fresh vegetables
1 loaf Italian bread, cut in 1-inch slices

1. Press minced garlic against side of FONDUE PAN with back of spoon to extract oil.
2. Add butter; bring to a simmer on range over medium heat.
3. Add anchovies; simmer slowly over low heat until anchovies lose their shape.
4. Slowly stir in olive oil; bring to a simmer.
5. Place FONDUE PAN on stand; light alcohol burner; adjust burner to have 3 small holes closed. (Sauce should simmer slowly.)
6. Eight servings as hors d'oeuvre. Four servings as entrée.

To Serve:

Provide each guest with salad plate, FONDUE FORK, regular fork. Arrange vegetables attractively on a platter; place platter, bread on table near FONDUE PAN. Each guest spears a vegetable on a FONDUE FORK and swirls it in the hot sauce. He then transfers it to a regular fork or to a slice of bread.

Suggested Fresh Vegetables:

Lettuce, small whole leaves
Cabbage, small whole leaves
Celery, cut in 2 x ½-inch strips
Green pepper, cut in 2 x ½-inch strips
Carrots, cut in 2 x ½-inch strips
Cucumber, seeded, cut in 2 x ½-inch strips
Green onions, in 2-inch lengths
Mushrooms, small whole
Cherry tomatoes

Meat Ball Fondue

2 pounds ground round
½ teaspoon salt
⅛ teaspoon onion salt
⅛ teaspoon pepper
¼ pound Cheddar or Swiss cheese
2 cups (1 pint) vegetable oil
Variety of sauces and side dishes

1. Combine meat, salt, onion salt, pepper; form in balls about ¾ inch in diameter.
2. Cut cheese into small cubes about ¼ inch using TRIMMER; insert cheese cube in center of each meatball; arrange on platter with lettuce; garnish with parsley.
3. Heat oil to 400° F. in FONDUE PAN on range over medium-high heat.
4. Place FONDUE PAN on stand; place adapter in pan; light alcohol burner; adjust burner to have 3 small holes closed.
5. Eight–ten servings as hors d'oeuvre.
Four–five servings as entrée.

To Serve:

Provide each guest with salad plate, FONDUE FORK, regular fork. Arrange meatballs attractively on a platter; place platter, sauces and accompaniments on table near FONDUE PAN. Each guest spears a meatball on a FONDUE FORK and cooks it in the hot oil. He then transfers his meatball to a regular fork and dips it into the sauce of his choice.

Sauces:

Tomato Sauce
Curry Sauce
Tartar Sauce

Accompaniments:

Hot and mild mustards
Ketchup
Mixed pickles

Variations:

Cubes of onion, green pepper, mushroom, water chestnut may be substituted for cheese.

Fondue Chocolat

2 9-ounce milk chocolate candy bars
2 1-ounce squares unsweetened baking chocolate
1 cup light cream
3 tablespoons kirsch, cognac or Cointreau

1. Break chocolate candy bars and baking chocolate into pieces; place in FONDUE PAN.
2. Add cream, kirsch.
3. Place on range over low heat until chocolate is melted, mixture is smooth; stir constantly using MIX-STIR.
4. Place FONDUE PAN on stand; light alcohol burner; adjust burner to have all 6 small holes closed.
5. Eight–ten servings for snack. Four–five servings for dessert.

To Serve:
Provide each guest with a salad plate, FONDUE FORK and regular fork. Place dishes of dunkables on table near FONDUE PAN.

To Eat:
Each guest spears a dunkable on the FONDUE FORK, then swirls it through the chocolate, transferring the coated dunkable to regular fork.
Flame beneath the pan should be kept regulated so that the fondue bubbles lightly.

Suggested Dunkables:
Fresh Fruits
  tangerine or orange sections
  pineapple, pear, peach, banana chunks
  grapes, strawberries, cherries
Canned fruits, well drained
Angel food cake, cut in chunks
Doughnuts, cut in chunks
Marshmallows, popcorn

Fondue Chocolateen

Prepared the same as the Fondue Chocolat except that ½ teaspoon ground cinnamon and ½ teaspoon ground cloves should be substituted for the kirsch. Follow the same serving, eating and dunkable suggestions.

Butterscotch Fondue

2 12-ounce jars butterscotch ice cream topping
2 tablespoons butter or margarine
Assorted dunkables

1. Heat butterscotch topping, butter in FONDUE PAN on range until butter melts.
2. Place FONDUE PAN on stand; light alcohol burner; adjust burner to have all 6 small holes closed.
3. Eight servings as snack. Four servings as dessert.

Follow the Fondue Chocolat serving, eating and dunkable suggestions.

Apple Cheddar Fondue

2 tablespoons butter or margarine
3 tablespoons flour
1 cup milk
½ pound Cheddar cheese, grated
Dash salt
Sliced green apples

1. Melt butter in FONDUE PAN on range over medium heat; add flour, stirring until well blended using MIX-STIR.
2. Gradually add milk, stirring constantly; cook several minutes over low heat.
3. Add cheese by handfuls, stirring constantly until cheese melts; add salt.
4. Place FONDUE PAN on stand; light alcohol burner; adjust burner to have all 6 small holes closed.
5. Eight–ten servings as snack. Four–five servings as dessert.

To Serve:
Provide each guest with a salad plate, FONDUE FORK, regular fork. Place tray of sliced apples on table near FONDUE PAN. Each guest spears a slice of apple on the FONDUE FORK. He dunks the apple in the fondue in a stirring motion to coat, then transfers it to a regular fork.

Outdoor Cooking

BUILDING THE FIRE

The easiest way is to spray the charcoal with any one of several good fire starters to be found on the market, following the instructions on the container. Only a sheet of newspaper is needed for igniting and the coals are ready in ten to fifteen minutes. As a rule, less charcoal is needed because a single layer is sufficient for most charcoal broiling.

When the coals have all turned white on top and you can see a steady red glow underneath, the fire is ready. For best results, don't rush this preparation time. Flames, even little ones, do nothing but scorch the meat, spoiling the true charcoal flavor. It's better to be hungry a little longer than to serve meat resembling a piece of charred wood.

ALCOA WRAP A MUST

Heavy Duty Alcoa Wrap is practically indispensable in Outdoor Cookery.

A sheet of foil accordion pleated into one-inch pleats, placed under the charcoal, reflects the heat. The charcoal can be placed about an inch apart—thus less charcoal is needed.

When doing meat on the rotisserie, make the drip pan from Heavy Duty Alcoa Wrap. It catches all the fat and can be tossed away later.

For greater heat reflectivity, line sides and top of Barbecue with Heavy Duty Alcoa Wrap; also makes cleaning easier.

Shape double thick squares of Heavy Duty Alcoa Wrap into little bowls for holding sauces or garlic butter brushed onto meat during cooking. No pans to wash later.

Corn on the cob and potatoes, snugly wrapped in foil, may be cooked right in the coals; turn several times. Fresh or frozen vegetables, wrapped in Heavy Duty Alcoa Wrap can be done on the grill; turn packages several times to insure even cooking.

When cooking for a crowd and the grill is not large enough to cook all the meat at one time, keep the cooked batches hot by wrapping them in foil.

Use Heavy Duty Alcoa Wrap to keep corn on the cob and rolls hot during serving. Covering serving platters with foil eliminates dishwashing later.

OUTDOOR SMOKE OVEN COOKERY

This is the simplest and easiest method of Outdoor Cooking. While the food cooks you are free to enjoy your guests. The result, the most delicious meat, fish or fowl you ever tasted, all delicately seasoned with a true smoky flavor.

Any outdoor Barbecue or Grill can be converted into a Smoke Oven by making a Hood from Alcoa Wrap.

Here's how:

1. Before starting the fire, completely line the bowl or fire box with double-thick sheets of Heavy Duty Alcoa Wrap, allowing each strip to extend about three inches over the rim. Depending on size, you will have one to three double-thick sheets running from north to south and one to three double-thick sheets running from east to west.

2. Press overhang tightly to form a firm rim. The Hood now looks like an umbrella. Remove from bowl or fire box.

3. Cut a hole about 2 inches in diameter in the center of the top. This makes the vent necessary for good browning.

4. The Hood is now ready to use. It can be used over and over again —any time you want to do Smoke Oven Cookery.

To Do Smoke Oven Cookery:

1. Line fire box or bowl with Alcoa Wrap.

2. Build fire in usual way; put grill in place.

3. When coals start to turn gray, set a portable oven thermometer on the grill; cover with the Alcoa Wrap Hood; let Smoke Oven pre-heat to desired temperature.

4. Prepare food according to recipe; place on grill; add Hood; bake as directed in recipe.

GOOD TO KNOW: Alcoa Wrap Hood may be removed by inserting the tines of a barbecue fork into the vent. If Smoke Oven gets too hot, prop Hood up slightly.

BARBECUE SET

The long handled TONGS, TURNER and FORK are essential for the many turning and lifting jobs around the outdoor grill.

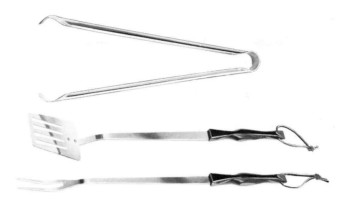

ACCESSORIES

While you will find the Barbecue Shop in any store well stocked with all kinds of tricky gadgets, there are only a few that are really necessary. Start with these and then let your continued interest in outdoor cookery be your guide on future purchases.

Gloves—A pair of heavy canvas work gloves are indispensable for handling the charcoal when starting the fire. Asbestos gloves are good to have for adjusting the spit, moving hot coals when additional charcoal needs to be added or for other hot jobs.

Sprinkling Bottle—A large bottle with a sprinkler such as is used for sprinkling clothes is needed to extinguish flames that flare up during broiling.

Sauce Brush—A regular pastry brush with a fairly long handle is necessary for brushing meats either when broiling or doing meat on the spit.

Thermometers—A regular meat thermometer goes a long way toward doing a perfect roast over the grill. Knowing the right internal temperature is the only sure way of knowing the roast is done to your liking. An oven thermometer is necessary when using a Smoke Oven in order that it can be preheated to the proper temperature.

Hinged Broilers—Several of these with medium to fine grids are convenient for broiling bacon, chicken livers, oysters, tidbits, shrimp, etc.

Skewers—These should be 12–18 inches long and preferably of a non-rusting metal. They are desirable for all kinds of skewered foods.

Wire Brush—A stiff wire brush, resembling a regular scrubbing brush in size and shape, makes the cleaning of the grill an easy task.

CHARCOAL ROTISSERIE TIME CHARTS

	Thermometer Reading	Approximate Time
Beef		
Standing Rib		
Rare	140° F.	2–2½ hours
Medium	140°–150° F.	2½–3 hours
Well Done	160°–170° F.	3–4 hours
Rolled Rib: Allow about 25–35 minutes longer. Thermometer reading will be the same.		
Lamb		
Leg		
Medium	150°–160° F.	1½–2 hours
Well Done	175°–180° F.	2–2½ hours
Boned Shoulder: Same as for leg of lamb.		
Pork		
Fresh Loin	170°–175° F.	2–2½ hours
Fresh Ham—12 pounds	170°–175° F.	4 hours
Veal		
Rolled Roast—3 pounds	165°–170° F.	45–60 minutes

	Weight	Approximate Time
Poultry		
Chicken	3–4 lbs.	1–1½ hours
Turkey	15 lbs.	3–4 hours
Duck	4–6 lbs.	1–1½ hours
Goose	4–7 lbs.	1¾–2½ hours
Rabbit	3–5 lbs.	40 min.–2 hours
Wild Duck	1–2½ lbs.	20–30 minutes
Cornish Hens	1–2 lbs.	1–1½ hours

ROTISSERIE ROASTED MEATS

1. Start charcoal fire early to have coals burning evenly for a low, steady heat.
2. Wipe meat with damp cloth; rub with cut side of clove of garlic; sprinkle with salt, pepper.
3. Insert spit rod completely through center of meat; insert spit fork into each end; tighten screws.
4. Check meat for balance by rotating spit between palms of hands.
5. If using a meat thermometer, insert it into thickest part, being sure bulb does not rest on bone, fat or gristle.

6. Arrange charcoal briquettes at back of fire box; knock off the gray ash.
7. Place a drip pan fashioned from heavy duty Alcoa Wrap in front of the coals.
8. Attach spit; start motor, having fire box at highest position until meat is seared.
9. Lower fire box 6–7 inches; continue roasting.
10. Roast according to Rotisserie Chart.

CHARCOAL BROILING TIME CHART

	Thickness	Rare	Medium	Well Done
Beef				
Steaks	1 inch	8–12 min.	12–15 min.	15–20 min.
	1½ inches	10–15 min.	14–18 min.	18–25 min.
	2 inches	18–30 min.	25–30 min.	45–60 min.
	2½ inches	30–35 min.	35–45 min.	60–75 min.
Hamburgers			14–15 min.	18–20 min.
Lamb				
Chops, steaks	1 inch		6–14 min.	18–25 min.
	1½ inches		8–16 min.	20–30 min.
	2 inches		12–20 min.	25–30 min.

	Thickness	Time
Pork		
Chops, steaks	1 inch	25–35 minutes
	1½ inches	30–45 minutes
Ham Steaks	¾ inch	25–30 minutes
	1 inch	30–35 minutes
	1½ inches	35–45 minutes
	2 inches	45–60 minutes
Poultry		
Chicken	Split	25–45 minutes
Duck	Split	30–50 minutes
Squab	Split	25–35 minutes
Fish		
Fish Steaks	1 inch	6–9 minutes
	1½ inches	8–12 minutes
	2 inches	10–18 minutes
Fish Fillets		6–18 minutes
Split Fish	Small	8–12 minutes
Whole Fish	Small	12–18 minutes
Whole Fish	Large	30–60 minutes

Outdoor Cooking

Chuck Steak Aruba

Juice of 2 large lemons
¼ cup olive oil
2 tablespoons grated onion
1 tablespoon chili powder
2 teaspoons ginger
1 clove garlic, mashed to a pulp
1 tablespoon salt
1 chuck steak, 1-inch thick

1. Combine lemon juice, oil, onion, chili powder, ginger, garlic, salt; blend thoroughly using MIX-STIR.
2. Place steak in shallow pan; pour marinade over meat; turn so both sides are coated; cover pan with Alcoa Wrap; refrigerate overnight or at least 10 hours; spoon marinade over steak several times using SOLID SPOON.
3. Place on grill over very hot coals, approximately 5–7 minutes per side; have coals as close to meat as possible.
4. Heat remaining marinade; use as sauce with meat.
5. Carve steak using PETITE CARVER.
6. Four servings.

Variation: Use ¾ cup bottled Italian Salad Dressing as marinade.

Fish Barbecue

2 1-pound packages frozen fish fillets
Prepared barbecue sauce

1. Allow fish to defrost enough to separate fillets.
2. Divide fillets into six servings.
3. Place each serving in center of double thick square of Alcoa Wrap.
4. Brush each fillet generously with a favorite barbecue sauce.
5. Bring up sides of Alcoa Wrap; fold down onto fish in tight double fold; fold ends up in tight double folds.
6. Place packages on grill over medium coals; grill 20–25 minutes.
7. Serve in opened foil packages.
8. Six servings.

Marinated Lobster Tails

6 tablespoons lemon juice
1½ tablespoons soy sauce
½ teaspoon ginger
½ teaspoon salt
½ teaspoon tarragon
½ teaspoon Tabasco sauce
1 cup sherry wine
1 clove garlic
8 frozen lobster tails, thawed

1. Combine lemon juice, soy sauce, ginger, salt, tarragon, Tabasco, sherry; blend well using MIX-STIR.
2. Finely mince garlic clove using FRENCH CHEF'S KNIFE; add to marinade.
3. Cut under-shell around edge of lobster tails with KITCHEN SHEARS; remove membrane.
4. Place lobster tails in shallow bake pan; pour marinade over lobster; cover pan with Alcoa Wrap; refrigerate several hours or overnight; spoon marinade over lobster several times using SOLID SPOON.
5. Preheat charcoal grill with Alcoa Wrap Smoke Oven Hood to 350° F.
6. Remove lobster tails from marinade; place directly on grill above charcoal with shell side down on grill; add Hood; grill 6–9 minutes, basting occasionally with marinade.
7. Four servings.

Herb Lamb Chops

1 medium onion
6 large sprigs parsley
1 cup olive oil
½ cup lemon juice
1½ teaspoons salt
1½ teaspoons marjoram
1½ teaspoons thyme
¾ teaspoon pepper
¼ teaspoon garlic salt
6 shoulder lamb chops, ½-inch thick

1. Peel onion using PARING KNIFE; chop using FRENCH CHEF'S KNIFE.
2. Snip parsley using KITCHEN SHEARS.
3. Combine onion, parsley, olive oil, lemon juice, salt, marjoram, thyme, pepper, garlic salt; blend well using MIX-STIR.
4. Place lamb chops in shallow bake pan; pour marinade over chops; cover pan with Alcoa Wrap; refrigerate several hours or overnight; spoon marinade over chops several times using SOLID SPOON.
5. Preheat charcoal grill with Alcoa Wrap Smoke Oven Hood to 350° F.
6. Remove chops from marinade; place directly on grill above charcoal; add Hood; grill 8 minutes per side.
7. Heat marinade; serve with grilled chops.
8. Six servings.

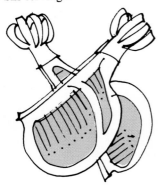

Grilled Lamb Steaks

4 lamb steaks from leg, 1-inch thick
¾ cup olive oil
¼ cup vinegar
1 clove garlic, mashed to a pulp
1 teaspoon salt
¼ teaspoon pepper
½ teaspoon crushed dried mint

1. Place steaks in shallow baking pan.
2. Combine oil, vinegar, garlic, salt, pepper, mint; blend well using MIX-STIR; pour over steaks.
3. Cover pan with Alcoa Wrap; refrigerate 3–4 hours, turning once.
4. Preheat charcoal grill with Alcoa Wrap Smoke Oven Hood to 350° F.
5. Remove steaks from marinade; place directly on grill above charcoal; add Hood; grill 10–12 minutes per side; baste frequently with marinade.
6. Four servings.

Smothered Onions

1 medium onion
1 tablespoon butter or margarine
Salt, pepper

1. Peel onion using PARING KNIFE; slice using TRIMMER.
2. Place sliced onion in center of double thick square of Alcoa Wrap.
3. Place butter on top; sprinkle with salt, pepper.
4. Bring up sides of Alcoa Wrap; fold down onto onions in tight double fold; fold ends up in tight double folds.
5. Place package on grill over medium coals; grill 25–30 minutes; turn package several times.
6. Serve in open package.
7. One serving.

Index

Index

N

O

P

Q

R

S

Index

D

Equivalents and Substitutions

Baking Powder		
Rising Equivalent	1 teaspoon	⅓ teaspoon baking soda plus ½ teaspoon cream of tartar
	1 teaspoon	¼ teaspoon baking soda plus ½ cup buttermilk
Bread Crumbs		
Dry	⅓ cup	1 slice
Soft	¾ cup	1 slice
Butter or Margarine		
1 stick	8 tablespoons	½ cup (¼ lb.)
4 sticks	2 cups	1 pound
Cheese, Cheddar	1 cup grated	¼ pound
Cheese, Cream	6 tablespoons	3-oz. package
Cheese, Cottage	1 cup	½ pound
Chocolate	1 square	1 ounce
Chocolate	1 square	4 tablespoons, grated
Chocolate	1 oz. plus 4 teaspoons sugar	1⅔ oz. semi-sweet chocolate
Cocoa	3 tablespoons cocoa plus 1 tablespoon fat	1 oz. chocolate
Coconut, fine grated	1 cup	3½ ounces
Coconut, flaked	1⅓ cups	3½ ounces
Cornstarch		
For thickening	1 tablespoon	2 tablespoons flour
Dates, pitted	1¼ cups cut-up	8-oz. package
Eggs, whole		
Large	5	about 1 cup
Medium	6	about 1 cup
Small	7	about 1 cup
Eggs, whites		
Large	8	about 1 cup
Medium	10-11	about 1 cup
Small	11-12	about 1 cup
Eggs, yolks		
Large	12	about 1 cup
Medium	13-14	about 1 cup
Small	15-16	about 1 cup
Flour		
All-purpose	1 cup sifted	1 cup plus 2 tablespoons cake flour
Cake	1 cup sifted	1 cup minus 2 tablespoons all-purpose flour